How to Start, Run, and Stay in Business

How to Start, Run, and Stay in Business
Second Edition

Gregory F. Kishel
Patricia Gunter Kishel

John Wiley & Sons, Inc.
New York • Chicester • Brisbane • Toronto • Singapore

Library of Congress Cataloging-in-Publication Data:

Kishel, Gregory F., 1946-
    How to start, run, and stay in business / by Gregory F. Kishel, Patricia Gunter Kishel. — Rev. and updated.
      p. cm. — (Wiley small business edition)
    Previous ed. published under title: Start, run, and profit from your own home-based business. 1991.
    Includes index.
    ISBN 0-471-59254-4 — ISBN 0-471-59255-2 (pbk.)
    1. Home-based businesses. 2. New business enterprises.
    I. Kishel, Patricia Gunter. 1948- . II. Kishel, Gregory F., 1946-
Start, run, and profit from your own home-based business.
III. Title. IV. Series.
HD62.7.K582 1993
658′.041—dc20   93-16708

Printed in the United States of America

10 9 8 7 6 5 4 3 2 1

Preface

Starting and operating your own business is one of the most exciting and potentially rewarding activities in which you can engage. In terms of your standard of living, as well as the level of your personal satisfaction, there's no limit to what you can achieve through private enterprise. To increase the probability of your success, our book provides the practical information every business owner needs—and presents it in a way that's easy to understand and ready to be utilized.

Many features make *How to Start, Run, and Stay in Business* equally suited for both prospective and present business owners.

Handbook format. Each stage of business operations—from selecting the right kind of business to financing, insuring, and promoting it—is covered on a chapter-by-chapter basis.

Checklists. These are included throughout the book so that you can measure your progress and monitor any areas of your business that need improvement.

Visual examples. Whether it's an accounting form, a job application, or a press release, you can *see* what it looks like.

Approach. The real-world approach to operating a business gives you the information you want when you need it.

Here are a few questions explored in the following chapters.

- How can I raise enough money to get started?
- What's the right kind of business for me?
- Which is better—a sole proprietorship, partnership, or corporation?
- How much insurance should I have?
- What's the best way to find good workers?
- How much should I charge?
- Can I afford to advertise right away?
- Do I need a complicated bookkeeping system?
- What's involved in purchasing a franchise?
- What if I get stuck and need outside help?

Whether you're thinking about starting your own business, or already running one, you'll find the answers you've been looking for in these pages.

More than 100,000 readers used the first edition of our book to start or build businesses of their own. Many took the time to thank us for writing the book and to share their stories with us. For this we are grateful. One entrepreneur told us that she kept the book next to her cash register and had used it so many times that the pages were falling out!

Now, with this updated and expanded edition of *How to Start, Run, and Stay in Business,* we look forward to helping the next generation of entrepreneurs. We wish you much success . . . and hope that our book finds a place next to *your* cash register.

Gregory F. Kishel
Patricia Gunter Kishel

Contents

5. Structuring the Business   41

Sole Proprietorship / Partnership / Corporation / Government Regulation / Structuring the Business Checklist

6. Recordkeeping   64

The Value of Good Records / Setting Up the Books / The Accounting Process / Recordkeeping Checklist

7. Financial Statements   77

Summarizing Financial Data / The Importance of Financial Statements / The Balance Sheet / The Income Statement / Interpreting Financial Data / Financial Ratio Checklist

8. Obtaining Capital   88

Determining Your Initial Investment / Sources of Capital / SBA Plan Questionnaire / Financing Checklist

9. Controlling Your Inventory   104

The Optimum Level of Inventory / Economic Order Quantity / Merchandise Turnover / Universal Product Codes / Just-in-Time Management / Inventory Shrinkage / Inventory Checklist

10. Setting the Price   114

Pricing and Customers / Pricing and Competition / Pricing and the Economy / Pricing and Profit / Pricing Methods / More About Markups / Pricing Strategy / Pricing Strategy Checklist

11. Staffing   124

Analyse Each Job / Prepare Job Descriptions / Check Recruitment Sources / Utilize Application Forms / Conduct Interviews / Verify Information / The Hiring Decision Is Made / Provide Job Orientation / Provide Training / Evaluate Performance / Compensate Employees / Monitor Employee Turnover / Staffing Checklist

12. Managing and Motivating   138

Developing Your Own Management Style / Knowing When to Delegate / Finding Ways to Motivate / Leadership Checklist

1

Getting Started

In any successful business operation the secret ingredient is planning. The adage that failing to plan means planning to fail is especially true of running a business. Without good plans, a business is totally at the mercy of fate, ruled by laws based on random probability, rather than sound judgment. In this situation, instead of you running your business, it runs you. The way to avoid this is by taking the time to formulate your objectives *before* starting your business. This entails analyzing your reasons for wanting to go into business in the first place, rating your abilities in different areas, and determining which kind of business best suits you.

WHAT'S IN IT FOR ME?

"What's in it for me?" is the first question you should ask yourself. Forming and operating your own business requires investments of money, time, and energy. In exchange for the opportunity of owning your own business, you give up the benefits that employees take for granted: job tenure, a regular paycheck, paid holidays, vacations, and sick leave, a company insurance plan; and the ability to leave your job behind at the end of the day. It's only logical that you should want to know what to expect in the form of a return on your investment—not just in dollars, but in satisfaction.

The advantages of owning a business. The number of new businesses started in the United States each year is currently growing at a faster rate than the population—clear evidence that owning a business is perceived as offering certain advantages. Those mentioned most often include:

- Control. The authority to make decisions rests with you. As the boss you have the power to direct all the activities of your business.

- Creative freedom. Without the restriction imposed by set policies and the need to go through channels, ideas and talent can be freely expressed.

- Profits. The more successful your business is, the more money you can make. Whereas employees' salaries are generally dependent on budget approvals and cost of living increases, yours is directly linked to performance.

- Job security. Since it's your business, you can't be fired, laid off, or forced to retire.

- Pride. There's the satisfaction that comes from knowing you have built your business into a successful operation through your own efforts.

The disadvantages of owning a business. Being the boss isn't without its disadvantages. Among those most frequently mentioned are these:

- Risk of investment. If the business fails you could lose your entire investment. In addition to this, your personal assets may be jeopardized.

- Long hours. Keeping your business going is rarely just a 9:00 to 5:00 proposition, especially in the beginning. Be prepared to put in 12-hour days to make it work.

- Income fluctuation. Instead of receiving a regular paycheck, your income is subject to the ups and downs of the business.

- Responsibility. The freedom to make decisions carries the burden of standing by them. If anything goes wrong, ultimately you're the one who's responsible.

- Pressure. There's always the pressure to please customers, meet your payroll and satisfy creditors' demands.

- **Regulations.** You must abide by federal, state and local laws, as well as the safety stipulations imposed by your insurance carrier.

Do the advantages of owning a business outweigh the disadvantages? That's something only you can determine. Just as some individuals can be happy only when working for themselves, others prefer to work for an employer. In planning your own business, it's important that you keep sight of your own needs and wants. Will owning a business enable you to satisfy them? And at a price you're willing to pay?

HOW SUITED AM I?

Do you have what it takes to own and operate your own business? It isn't a matter of how smart you are; it's more a matter of personality and behavior. Researchers have found that individuals who possess certain characteristics are more likely to succeed as business owners than those who lack these characteristics. Although there's no total agreement as to the characteristics that are the most important, those frequently cited include:

- **Motivation.** This is the drive (mentally and physically) to succeed, to accomplish the tasks of your own choosing, on your own terms.
- **Confidence.** This is the firm belief in your own capabilities and your chances of success.
- **Willingness to take risks.** This is the readiness to sacrifice your own security, if need be, in order to accomplish your goals.
- **Ability to make decisions.** This is the talent to analyze complex situations and draw the conclusions that will make your business succeed.
- **Human relations skills.** This is the ability to get along with others, to inspire cooperation, confidence, and loyalty.
- **Communications skills.** This is the ability to express yourself and to understand others, so that ideas can be shared.
- **Technical ability.** This is the expertise to produce the goods and services of your business.

To rate yourself in these areas and get some additional input regarding your suitability for the entrepreneurial role, read this **Rating Scale for Personal Traits Important to a Business Owner** and answer the questions as objectively as you can.

Instructions: After reading each question, circle the letter of the answer that fits you the best. Be honest with yourself.

1. **Are you a self-starter?**

   a. When something needs to be done, I do it. Nobody has to tell me.
   b. If someone gets me started, I keep on track.
   c. Easy does it. I don't put myself out unless I have to.

2. **How do you feel about other people?**

   a. I like people and can get along with just about anybody.
   b. I have plenty of friends. I don't need anyone else.
   c. People, in general, tend to irritate me.

3. **Can you lead others?**

   a. I can get most people to follow me without much difficulty.
   b. I can give the orders as long as someone tells me what to do.
   c. I usually let someone else get things moving, then join in if I want.

4. **Can you take responsibility?**

   a. I like to take charge and see things through.
   b. I can take charge if I have to, but I'd rather let someone else be responsible.
   c. Go-getters always want to show off. I say let them.

5. **Are you a good organizer?**

   a. I like to have a plan before I start. I'm usually the one to get things lined up.
   b. I'm pretty good, unless things get too complicated. Then I quit.
   c. I just take things as they come. It's easier that way.

6. **Are you a good worker?**

   a. I can keep going as long as necessary. I don't mind working hard.
   b. I'll work hard up to a point, but when I've had enough, that's it.
   c. I can't see that hard work gets you anywhere.

7. **Can you make decisions?**

   a. I can make up my mind when I need to, and my decisions usually turn out okay.
   b. I can if I have plenty of time. Otherwise I end up second-guessing myself.
   c. I don't like to be the one who decides things. There's too much pressure.

8. **Can people trust what you have to say?**

   a. They sure can. I don't say things I don't mean.
   b. I try to be on the level, but sometimes I just say what's easiest.
   c. I don't worry about the truth if the other person doesn't know the difference.

9. **Can you stick with it?**
   a. If I make up my mind to do something, I don't let anything stop me.
   b. I usually finish what I start.
   c. If a job doesn't go right, I bail out. Why beat your head against the wall?

10. **How good is your health?**
    a. I never run down.
    b. I have enough energy for most things I want to do.
    c. I'm okay as long as I don't try to do too much.

Where did most of your circles go? Ideally, letter *a* should have been your choice for each question. If it wasn't, then you have one or more weak spots to consider. It's up to you to find ways to bring about improvements in these areas, either by changing your personal habits and attitudes or by staffing your business with people whose strengths can augment yours.

Goal setting. One way to improve your chances for success is to set goals for accomplishing the various tasks associated with forming and operating your own business. For each goal you should indicate your plan of action and specify the target date for its achievement. Then, as each target date arrives, your actual performance can be compared with your intended performance. Whenever a goal is reached a new goal should be set. In this way you can keep both your momentum and your motivation going at a steady pace. For example, your list of goals might go like this:

Month 1

- Read *How to Start, Run, and Stay in Business.*
- Visit the Small Business Administration (SBA) and gather information on starting a business.
- Do research in the public library.

Month 2

- Decide on the type of business to start.
- Collect as much information as possible on the business.
- Attend one of the SBA's Prebusiness Seminars and any other relevant seminars.

Months 3-5

- Prepare a plan of action to obtain funds, locate and furnish business.

- Go over the plan with a counselor at the local Small Business Development Center.

Month 6

- Open business.

Year 1

- Have business break even.

Year 2

- Make a 15-percent profit on sales.

Years 3-5

- Open a second store.

For the goal-setting process to work, the goals that you set for yourself should be:

1. Measurable.
2. Scheduled.
3. Realistic.
4. In writing.

1. Measurable. It isn't enough just to say that you want to "do well" or to "be a success." You have to have a way to measure your goals. In other words, if you want to be a recognized leader in your field within three years, think of the criteria for judging whether you have attained the goal—membership in specific organizations, write-ups in newspapers and magazines, sales volume, and so on. Unless there is some standard of measurement that can be used to determine what constitutes a recognized leader, there's no way to know if you are one.

2. Scheduled. Each goal that you set for yourself should have a specific time frame for its completion. If you have to move a date up or push it back, you can. But having a completion date to shoot for will make it easier for you to schedule the work needed to accomplish the goal and to monitor your progress. Are you on schedule, behind schedule, or ahead of schedule?

3. Realistic. Setting unrealistic goals for yourself is just setting yourself up for failure. Few people become "overnight" millionaires or earn enough to retire within six months of starting their businesses. Look at what other business owners in your field have accomplished and how long it took them to do it. Then compare this to your own circumstances and set your goals accordingly. Keep in mind, too, that the closer your business goals are to your personal goals, the greater the likelihood that you will achieve both.

4. In writing. A goal that isn't in writing isn't a goal, as management experts will tell you. By writing down the things you want to accomplish, you help them to become real. Putting your goals in writing not only clarifies them, but enables you to keep them in focus as you work toward attaining them.

WHICH KIND OF BUSINESS?

Perhaps you have already selected the kind of business you would like to start. Or you may be considering several alternatives. In either case, how can you tell if you've picked a winner? Will your proposed business be able to support you both materially and emotionally? This depends on such difficult-to-predict factors as the economy, competition, resources, and the political environment—all of them forces beyond your control. But it also depends on another factor that you *can* control—yourself. And this factor must be as carefully considered as the others. A business that's right for a friend of yours may not be right for you. Unless you select a type of business, or a field, that genuinely appeals to you, the odds on your winning are so slight that you're better off not leaving the starting gate.

To shift the odds in your favor, the first thing you should do during the business planning stage is think about what you really want to do. Try to come up with ideas for businesses that you would actually enjoy running, not just to make money but to have fun doing it. The more ideas the better. And as you come up with an idea, *write it down.* Once you start digging into your own background, experience, education, and hobbies for inspiration, you may be surprised at how many different businesses appeal to you.

After you've expanded your list to the limit, the next step is to narrow it down, focusing on those business opportunities that most closely match your own qualifications. For instance, if you have a fear of heights and have never jumped out of a plane, a skydiving school is probably a poor choice for you. If, on the other hand, you're a dedicated amateur photographer and enjoy trying out new camera gadgetry and dealing with people, a camera shop may be an excellent choice.

If you're determined to start a specific business, even though you know very little about it, what can you do to minimize your risk? Find out as much as possible about your intended business before attempting to open it. This can be done by getting additional education, taking a job in someone else's business, researching the business in the library, talking to people in the field, and so on. Even though this may make you postpone opening your doors, the delay will be worth it. Once your doors are open, you'll be in a better position to *keep* them open.

As for those uncontrollable factors that also affect your business, the best way to cope with them is to stay tuned in to what's happening in each area. Some new business owners get so caught up in their own affairs that they fail to keep track of events that may have a direct bearing on their operations. You can avoid this by reading newspapers and magazines, listening to what people have to say, and observing the changes in your environment.

CHECKLIST FOR GOING INTO BUSINESS

Now that you have thought about your reasons for going into business, examined your temperament, and considered the opportunities open to you, the checklist should help you to get started. The questions in it relate to both the formation and the actual operation of your own business. Answer each question yes or no. Be as honest with yourself as you can. This will help you find weaknesses that need improvement and topics that you need to research further.

Before You Start	Answer Yes or No
About you	
Are you the kind of person who can get a business started and make it go?	_____
Do you want to own your own business badly enough to keep working long hours without any guarantee that it will succeed?	_____
Have you ever worked in a business like the one you want to start?	_____
Have you ever worked as a supervisor or manager?	_____
Have you had any business training in school?	_____

Before You Start	Answer Yes or No
Have you researched your proposed business and tried to learn as much about it as possible?	_____

About money

Have you saved any money to invest in a business?	_____
Do you know how much money you will need to get your business started?	_____
Do you know how much credit you can get from your suppliers—the people you will buy from?	_____
Do you know where you can borrow the rest of the money you need?	_____
Have you figured out what your annual net income (salary plus profits) will be?	_____
Can you live on less than this amount, if necessary?	_____
Have you talked to a banker about your plans?	_____

About a partner

If you need a partner with the money or the know-how that you don't have, is there someone available you could work with?	_____
Do you know the pros and cons of going it alone, having a partner, or incorporating your business?	_____
Have you talked to a lawyer about your options?	_____

About customers

Have you identified a niche for yourself in the marketplace?	_____
Is there a need for your particular product or service?	_____
Do you know who your customers will be?	_____
Do you understand their needs and wants?	_____
Will your product offering be competitive in all aspects—price, quality, etc.?	_____
Have you chosen a location that is convenient for your customers?	_____

Getting Started

Your building

Have you found a suitable building for your business?	_____
Will you have enough room when your business grows?	_____

Getting Started	**Answer Yes or No**

Can you fix the building the way you want it without spending too much money?

Will there be adequate parking, maintenance, security, or other necessary support services?

Have you had a lawyer check the lease and zoning?

Equipment and supplies

Do you know what equipment and supplies you need and how much they will cost?

Can you save money by buying secondhand equipment?

Have you compared the difference between buying and leasing?

Your merchandise

Have you decided what merchandise to carry?

Do you know how much inventory you will need on opening day?

Have you found suppliers who will sell you what you need at a good price?

Have you compared the prices and credit terms of different suppliers?

Your records

Have you chosen a recordkeeping system that will keep track of your income and expenses, assets, and liabilities?

Have you worked out a way to keep track of your inventory so that you will have enough on hand for your customers, but not more than you can sell?

Have you figured out how to maintain your payroll records and take care of tax reports and payments?

Do you know what financial statements you should prepare?

Do you know how to use these financial statements?

Your business and the law

Do you know what licenses and permits you need?

Do you know what business laws you have to obey?

Do you know a lawyer who can give you advice and help with legal papers?

Getting Started	Answer Yes or No

Protecting your business

Are you aware of the various risks that you should guard against? _____

Have you talked with an insurance agent about what kinds of insurance you need? _____

Have you made plans for protecting your business against thefts of all kinds—shoplifting, robbery, burglary, employee stealing? _____

When buying a business

Have you made a list about what you like and don't like about buying a business that someone else has started? _____

Are you sure you know the real reason the owner wants to sell the business? _____

Have you compared the cost of buying the business with the cost of starting a new business? _____

Is the inventory up-to-date and in good condition? _____

Is the building in good condition? _____

Will the owner of the building transfer the lease to you? _____

Have you talked with others in the area to see what they think of the business? _____

Have you talked with the company's suppliers? _____

Have you talked with a lawyer about the purchase? _____

Making It Go

Advertising

Have you decided how you will advertise (newspapers, magazines, direct mail, radio, etc.)? _____

Do you know where to get help with your ads? _____

Have you observed the types of promotion used by your competitors? _____

Pricing

Do you know how to calculate what you should charge for each item you sell? _____

Do you know what other businesses like yours charge? _____

Making It Go	Answer Yes or No
Buying	
Do you know what suppliers you intend to buy from?	_____
Will your plan for keeping track of your inventory tell you what and when to buy?	_____
Selling	
Do you know what selling techniques to use?	_____
Have you thought about the reasons people buy, and how you can convince customers to buy from you?	_____
Are you fully aware of the benefits associated with the products or service you will sell?	_____
Your employees	
If you need to hire someone to help you, do you know where to look?	_____
Do you know what kind of person you need?	_____
Do you know how much to pay?	_____
Do you have a plan for training your employees?	_____

A Few Extra Questions	
Will owning a business enable you to achieve your goals?	_____
Have you talked it over with your family and gotten their support?	_____
Are you willing to make the commitment to "be the boss"?	_____
Are you ready to begin developing your business plan?	_____

For every yes answer you gave, think of yourself as one step closer to turning your business dream into a reality. Each no answer represents an area to work on—a temporary roadblock, yes, but a deadend only if you let it be.

2

Preparing Your Business Plan

Given the rapid changes occurring in the marketplace and the increasing levels of competition that all businesses face, you can't afford to proceed blindly, hoping that hard work alone will be enough to make your business a success. To succeed, a business must have clearly defined objectives and a fully developed strategy for achieving them. In short, what's needed is a business plan.

Far from viewing a business plan as a luxury reserved for big businesses or as something created solely to impress the financial community, entrepreneurs should see it for what it is—one of the most important tools a business can have. Just as an organization chart shows the working relationships of the people within a business, a business plan shows the purpose of the business and what it intends to accomplish. A good business plan helps to give form and substance to an entrepreneurial vision, providing a mechanism that enables owners, managers, and workers alike to function effectively. The better the business plan, the better equipped your business will be to recognize and assess the opportunities and risks that lie ahead.

WHEN TO USE A BUSINESS PLAN

Much like a Swiss Army knife, with its multitude of tools and utensils, your business plan can serve many purposes. Among the times that your business plan should be of the greatest use to you are when you're:

1. Starting your business.
2. Expanding your business.
3. Developing new products.
4. Obtaining financing.
5. Making management decisions.
6. Maintaining control.

Starting Your Business

During the start-up stage of a business, the existence of a sound business plan can mean the difference between success and failure. Rather than pursuing conflicting goals or allowing the business to develop haphazardly, you can use the plan to keep your business on track.

Some of the questions your plan should answer are:

- What business am I in?
- What are my products or services?
- Who are my competitors?
- Who is my target market?
- What's the best marketing strategy?
- How should my resources be utilized?
- What is the business's profit potential?

Even though you may not be able to work out all the answers in advance or may find that they change later, the important thing is to have a set of assumptions about the business and its environment that you can share with others. This will make it easier for you to enlist their support in launching the business and in carrying out their respective tasks and yours as a cohesive unit.

Expanding Your Business

Your business plan can also help reduce the added risks involved in expanding your business. A plan is especially critical during an expansion phase since this is one of the most dangerous times for a business. If a business tries to expand too quickly before mastering its current level of activity, the quality of its products and services often suffers. On the other hand, if it waits too long, the market could already be saturated with similar product offerings and the opportunity may be lost.

By addressing such issues as *timing*, the *rate* of expansion (should the business grow at an annual rate of 5 percent or 20 percent?) and the *type* of expansion (a bigger building? additional locations? new products?), your plan can help you to make the right choices. In this way, instead of being overwhelmed by growth, you should be able to keep it at a manageable level.

Developing New Products

For most businesses the need to develop new products is a fact of life brought about by the continuing challenge to satisfy their customers. To remain competitive, your business must be able to anticipate and respond to customers' changing needs and to make effective use of new technologies. The way to accomplish this is by developing new products and services or by improving existing ones. The company that developed the electronic light bulb knew this; they invented a product that lasts years longer than traditional incandescent and fluorescent bulbs, and is more energy-efficient too.

Unless a business has a plan to guide it, though, the chances of its coming up with profitable ideas for new products, product modifications, or improvements are minimal. To make the most of your resources as your business grows, you must have a systematic plan for developing new products and managing your current ones.

Obtaining Financing

Commercial lenders, such as banks and finance companies, expect to see a business plan as a matter of course before they will lend money to a business. The same holds true for government lenders. Even when there is sufficient collateral to pledge as security for the loan, a business plan is still likely to be required because it shows where the business is going and how the money will be utilized.

A business plan is even more important if you're seeking investment capital. Investors, especially venture capitalists, tend to be more demanding than lenders because their risks are greater. Unless a plan can convince them that financing a business will enable them to earn a substantial return on their investment, the standard response is, "No go. No dough." This puts the burden on you to demonstrate through your business plan that the investment will be worth their while.

Making Management Decisions

Perhaps the most valuable use of a business plan is in making management decisions. By stating what the business wants to accomplish and assessing both its internal and external environments, a business plan shows the "big picture." This gives entrepreneurs a real advantage. Instead of operating in the dark or looking at just one aspect of a problem, they can consider it from all points of view and make the decision that is in the best overall interests of the business.

Along with this, your business plan can also help you to maintain your objectivity, enabling you to see the business as an outsider would. Putting sentiment aside, you can then focus on what needs to be done to achieve your goals, making hard decisions when necessary.

Maintaining Control

Another key use of a business plan is as a control device. Are goals being met? Did sales reach their target? Is production capacity increasing according to schedule? Are costs staying in line? Is the business doing what it set out to do?

You should be able to get the answers to these questions and more by examining your business plan. Then, by carefully rating your performance against your goals, you can determine if you're moving ahead or merely moving in place. If a method or strategy isn't working, or if you find that the business is going in a different direction, you can act quickly to bring things back in line or to chart a new course.

THE PLAN

Once you've made up your mind about what kind of business to start and have done your preliminary research, you're ready to begin preparing your business plan. Much as you may be tempted to skip this step or hire someone else to do the work for you, *don't*. The effort you put into it will be more than compensated later when your business is operational. And the knowledge you gain from creating the finished, written plan will be invaluable.

Although every business plan is different, reflecting the ideas and intentions of the person who wrote it, certain elements, or sections, are common to all plans. As shown in the Business Plan Outline that follows, your plan should be organized so that it provides essential information in a concise and logical format.

Business Plan Outline

- Title Page
- Table of Contents
- Executive Summary
- Business/Industry Description
- Product or Service Description
- Organizational Data
- Marketing Strategy
- Competitive Analysis
- Operations Plan
- Financial Information

Title Page

The title page should include the name of your business, its address and phone number, and the names of all owners. If your business is still at the idea stage, then use your own address and phone number for the time being. The important thing is to provide prospective lenders, investors, and others who see the plan with a means of contacting you.

Table of Contents

A table of contents is absolutely essential. It not only provides an overview of what's in your plan, but enables readers to quickly find what they're looking for without having to thumb through all the pages. This makes for a more "reader-friendly" plan, which will, in turn, help to generate a favorable response.

Executive Summary

The executive summary is the single most important element of a business plan. Having the power to make or break your plan, it should provide a concise, but clear, picture of your business—within a maximum of two pages. Designed to stimulate a busy reader's

interest, the executive summary's job is to convince the reader to take
the time to go over the rest of the plan in detail.

Among the points that you should cover in the executive summary are:

1. The current status of your business, indicating when it was started
   or it is expected to commence operations.
2. A description of your products or services.
3. Information about your target market and your means for reaching it.
4. The strengths inherent in your business that will enable it to
   achieve its objectives (i.e., experience, a unique idea, good location,
   product quality, and so on).
5. Your short-term and long-term plans.
6. Financial projections.
7. The amount of money, if any, you're currently seeking.

Condensing all this data to a two-page summary isn't easy. But,
by staying focused on the key facts, you can do it. And remember
that, even though the summary comes first in your business plan,
write it last. That way you'll have the business in perspective and the
information you need in hand.

Business/Industry Description

This section should begin with a statement of the business's goals
and objectives, defining what the business does (or will do) and its
purpose. This is the place to put background information about the
founding of the business, its ownership and legal structure, the nature of its industry, and the role the business intends to play in it. You
should also include any data you have about changes in the
marketplace that will lead to an increased demand for what your
business has to offer. As you can imagine, investors are particularly
attracted to growth industries.

Product or Service Description

Explain what your business sells or proposes to sell, describing your
product or services in detail: their features, quality and performance
levels, functions, and so on. Here it's important to point out what

separates them from competitors' product offerings and the benefits customers will derive from them. In other words, what makes your products or services unique or gives them the edge? If you are utilizing a trade secret (such as a recipe or formula) or have (or expect to receive) patent protection, that should also be stated.

Organizational Data

In this section you should outline the duties and responsibilities of the people involved in your business. You want to make it clear who does what (in production, sales, accounting, and so on) and who reports to whom. If you're currently an organization of one, describe the tasks you will be carrying out and estimate your future personnel needs. To further illustrate how your business is set up, it's a good idea to include an *organization chart* in this section, along with *resumes* showing each person's qualifications.

Marketing Strategy

The main reason for starting a business is to sell something. That's where marketing strategy comes in. The primary objectives in this section of your business plan are to:

1. Define your *target market*, describing your potential customers and why they buy.
2. Estimate the total *market size* and determine what share of it you can realistically hope to obtain.
3. Develop a *pricing structure* that will ensure you maximum profitability.
4. Determine what combination of *advertising and publicity* to use to promote the business.
5. Outline a *distribution strategy* that will enable you to reach customers in the most efficient way possible.

In spelling out these objectives, try to be as specific as you can, basing your marketing strategy on facts, rather than on wishful thinking. Much of the information you'll need to formulate your strategy can be obtained through books, magazines, government reports, trade associations, and your own observations and research.

Competitive Analysis

Your competitive analysis should identify the key players in your industry and explain how your business can compete with them. Focusing on your strengths and advantages (as noted in your Product or Service Description), you want to show how you can capitalize on them to gain your desired market share. Your purpose isn't to belittle the competition. Rather, it's to point out: (1) the customers whose needs they are failing to serve properly, if at all, and (2) the limitations (such as being too large or having dated technology) that keep them from doing what you can do.

Operations Plan

This is the "nuts and bolts" section of your business plan—the place to describe how your product or service will actually be produced or delivered to the customer. Information about facilities, equipment, and supplies all goes in here. You should also explain what technologies, skills, and processes are required to do the job.

Financial Information

Last is the section of your plan that lenders and investors often consider to be the "heart" of it. Consisting of the financial data relevant to your business venture, this section should include your current financial statements (if the business is already established), as well as a projected:

- Income statement.
- Balance sheet.
- Cash flow statement.

Covering a period of one to three years, these projections are meant to provide a financial picture of your business, showing its expected revenues and expenses, assets, and liabilities.

Doing the work to come up with the financial data you need takes time, but with practice, you'll be surprised at how adept you become at "number crunching." To find out more about financial statements and how to prepare and use them, see Chapters 7 and 8.

GUIDELINES FOR SUCCESSFUL PLANNING

The following guidelines should help you to master the planning process and to become more proficient at preparing, updating, and using business plans.

1. Set aside time for planning. Recognizing the need to plan is one thing; allocating the time to do it can be another. Call it "planning phobia" or simply "procrastination." Whatever the case, for your business to succeed, you must spend sufficient time on planning.

2. Determine in advance what you want to accomplish. What is the purpose of the planning effort? To prepare a business plan for a new venture? To update an existing plan? To obtain financing? By identifying your specific planning goals, you can focus your attention on the key issues or activities that need to be addressed.

3. Make sure you have access to the necessary facts. Information is what fuels the planning process. To plan effectively, your information must be relevant, accurate, and up-to-date. This means having access to internal information, such as accounting records and sales reports, and external information, such as industry trends, consumer buying habits, and so on.

4. Coordinate your planning efforts with the efforts of others. Make sure that each person involved in the planning process knows what everyone else is doing. To avoid working at cross purposes— pursuing one planning objective while a partner or employee is pursuing another—your efforts must be coordinated. This is the only way to maintain harmony and ensure that the various goals set for the business are compatible.

5. Keep an open mind. To achieve the best results as a planner, it's important not to get locked into one approach to a problem or situation. Different strategies must be given a chance to develop and possible courses of action explored. Above all, let yourself be creative. Rather than starting out with a preconceived idea of what your business should do or not do, take the time to consider the alternatives.

6. Solicit input from others. Don't be afraid to ask for advice and to get others' viewpoints. As your business grows, this will become increasingly important. The planning process works best when it is a collaborative effort bringing together those responsible for creating the business plan with those who will be called upon to implement it.

7. *Review your business plan.* Once your business plan is finished, go over it to see that it clearly depicts your business and adequately states your intentions for it. Before implementing the plan, you want to make sure that it will enable you to achieve your objectives.

8. *Update the plan.* Business experts often recommend updating a business plan every six months. That way you can determine whether the plan is continuing to meet the needs of your business. As circumstances change or as new information becomes available, the plan should be updated accordingly.

9. *Make the plan accessible.* All too often business plans are kept from the very people who need to see them. Keeping proprietary information from your competitors makes sense; keeping it from your own people does not. For key employees to fully contribute their talents and abilities to the business, they must know what it stands for and where it's going.

10. *Use the plan.* Most important of all, you must *use* your business plan. A plan that's gathering dust on a shelf or that's buried in a filing cabinet can't do you any good. If your plan really *is* going to be the blueprint for a successful business, then you must put it to work.

PLANNING CHECKLIST

To evaluate how your planning efforts are going and to identify those areas that need work, answer these questions.

	Answer Yes or No
1. Have you developed a clear concept of what you want your business to be?	_____
2. Have you learned as much as possible about your business and its industry?	_____
3. Do you have the necessary information (financial data, marketing research, production requirements, and so on) to put together a business plan?	_____
4. Have you looked at other business plans (available at your local library or Small Business Development Center) to see how they were written?	_____
5. Are you willing to put in the necessary time to prepare a business plan?	_____
6. Have you talked about your plan with the people whose support you'll need and solicited their help with it?	_____
7. Have you taken steps to make the planning process inclusionary, rather than exclusionary, so that everyone involved in your business can contribute to it?	_____
8. Is planning an ongoing part of your business activities?	_____
9. Do you place as much importance on planning as you do on taking action?	_____
10. Is your mind open to new ways of doing things and new opportunities?	_____
11. Have you allowed yourself to be creative in forming a business vision that is uniquely your own?	_____
12. Is your business plan updated at least once a year?	_____
13. Do you currently have a business plan that you are satisfied with?	_____
14. Are you really using your plan as a tool in making management decisions and in shaping your business?	_____

3

Determining the Best Location

The location for your business is too important to be decided on casually or solely on the basis of personal preference. To do so is to invite disaster. Major corporations are well aware of this. When seeking to relocate or expand their facilities, big business leaders sometimes spend years weighing the pros and cons of various locations. In your case, spending that much time is probably not feasible or even advisable. However, the same scientific approach that works for big business can work for you.

CHOOSING THE COMMUNITY

When evaluating a particular community, ask yourself the following questions:

1. Is there a need for my product or service?
2. How many customers are there?
3. How strong is the competition?
4. Is the community prosperous enough to support my business?
5. What is the community's growth potential?
6. What kinds of people live there (age, income, interests, occupations)?

7. What are the restrictions on my type of business (licenses, zoning, local ordinances)?
8. Will my suppliers have ready access to me?
9. Is the local labor force both adequate and affordable?
10. Do I like the community enough to live and work in it?

1. Is there a need for my product or service? A generally approved business strategy is to find a need and fill it. Will your new or preexisting business be able to fill a need in the community? If not, a change must be made—either in the type of business you're considering or in the community.

2. How many customers are there? Is the number of potential customers large enough to justify locating your business in the community? The closer you are to your main market, the easier it will be to serve it.

3. How strong is the competition? Having determined that there is a market for your product or service, it's important not to overlook the competition. Do any businesses already have a foothold in the community? How many? What can you offer that will set your business apart from the rest? If yours is to be the first such business in the community, why haven't others already located there? Perhaps there is some drawback you may have overlooked.

4. Is the community prosperous enough to support my business? To determine the community's level of prosperity, take a close look at its economic structure. Is it based on manufacturing, retail, services, or a combination of these? Who are the major employers in the town? What kind of work do the employees perform? How much unemployment is there? Could layoffs in one sector result in an economic collapse—if a plant closes down, for example?

5. What is the community's growth potential? Are people moving into the community or leaving it? Some positive indicators of growth are land development projects, the presence of department stores and other major businesses, well-kept homes and storefronts, active citizens' groups such as a chamber of commerce and PTA, and adequate public services (health, education, safety, transportation).

6. What kinds of people live there? In addition to the size of the community's population, you should be concerned about its makeup. Is the average age 52 or 22? How much does a typical worker earn? What percentage of the community is married? Single? Divorced? What's the average number of children per household? This type of statistical information—called *demographics*—can be obtained from local census tracts and chambers of commerce. For an even more complete profile of the local residents, you might examine their lifestyles as well. What do they like to do in their spare time? Read? Ski? Sew? Garden? Are they politically conservative or liberal? Data of this nature—known as *psychographics*—tell about the inner workings of people, focusing on their activities, interests, and opinions. Such information can be obtained through questionnaires, interviews, and your own observations.

   7. What are the restrictions on my type of business? Each community has its own unique restrictions, instituted to either promote or discourage different types of businesses. In selecting your location, make sure that you are aware of these restrictions. If not, you could find yourself prohibited from obtaining business licenses, expanding your facilities, receiving deliveries, or maintaining certain hours of operation. By finding out ahead of time what to expect, you can avoid unpleasant surprises later.

   8. Will my suppliers have ready access to me? If you are considering settling in a remote, out-of-the-way locale, your privacy may come at a price. Unless your suppliers have ready access to you, you could end up unable to obtain necessary shipments or paying premium shipping costs. This will, of course, have a bearing on the merchandise you carry and the prices you charge for it.

   9. Is the local labor force both adequate and affordable? Whether labor is available and affordable depends on your type of business. If you're opening a diner, there's probably not much to worry about. Short-order cooks are fairly well distributed geographically. But finding the right chef for an exclusive French restaurant could be more of a problem. The more specialized or technical the work tasks are, the greater the difficulty in hiring the right people. And this difficulty increases as the number of workers to be employed increases. As for wages, these vary with the community's standard of living. Will budgetary factors necessitate your locating in a community where labor costs are lower?

   10. Do I like the community enough to live and work in it? Regardless of your answers to the first nine questions, if you can't say yes to this one, keep looking. Relying on personal preferences alone can be disastrous, but ignoring them altogether can be equally so. The location that is best for your business must also be right for you and your family.

Once you've answered these questions, you'll be in a much better position to rate a particular community's attractiveness. And you'll quickly see that an ideal location for one business can be totally wrong for another. A seaside resort, for instance, might just be the place to sell bathing suits, but a bad choice for a furniture store.

Selecting the community where you wish to locate is only half the location process. The second and equally important step is to select a site within the community.

CHOOSING THE SITE

Regardless of the type of business you are planning to start, be it a retail, wholesale, manufacturing, or service establishment, site selection will play an important role in its development. Evidence of this was found in a major study conducted by General Foods. The company wanted to know why certain grocery stores achieved greater profitability than others; so it compared seemingly identical stores carrying the same merchandise and utilizing the same operating and promotional procedures. Management effectiveness was also taken into consideration. Surprisingly enough, the stores that stood head and shoulders above the rest weren't always the best managed. Another factor was needed to explain this—the sites of the various stores. Because of errors in site selection, some of the stores, though well managed, could never hope to achieve the success of the stores with the better locations. Such liabilities as competition, declining neighborhoods, and inadequate parking space were just too much to overcome.

The success of Sears Roebuck after World War II can largely be attributed to its recognition of the importance of site selection. Instead of adding stores in the already overcrowded downtown areas of American cities, where other major retailers were focusing their efforts, Sears decided to open its new stores on the outskirts of the cities. This was where it anticipated the postwar families would want to live. To further meet these families' needs, Sears made it a point to provide adequate parking space as well—something its downtown competitors were unable to do.

THE ENVIRONMENT

The site for your business could be:

- The downtown business district.
- A shopping center.
- A major street.
- A side street.
- Near a highway access.
- An industrial/commercial park.
- A business incubator.

Each has its own unique characteristics, which you will want to consider. Then, given your particular business, you can select the environment that will be best suited to its needs.

The downtown business district. The downtown business district is the part of town where finance, business, and industrial concerns generally have their headquarters. Depending on the community in which you've decided to locate, this area can range in size from a few square blocks to many square miles. In this environment, a high percentage of your customers will be employees of the neighboring businesses. And, although they may commute great distances by car to reach their jobs, once there they will generally confine any shopping to what's within walking distance. Peak shopping times, not surprisingly, are during lunch and before and after work. In the evenings and on weekends, sales are likely to drop off. The businesses most likely to flourish in a city's downtown areas are restaurants, shoe stores, bars, department stores, gift stores, book stores, clothing shops, and any other enterprises that cater to the working person.

A shopping center. The development of planned shopping centers and malls, which reached a peak in the 1980s, changed forever the way people shop and businesses operate. Shoppers could now do their shopping in a controlled environment without having to leave, drive long distances between stores, or repeatedly search for parking places. Retail and service establishments could attract customers into their places of business simply by being in a popular shopping center or mall. Potential customers, who once might have driven by without stopping, now would stop to look and to buy.

Shopping centers clearly seemed to be the way to go—but not all centers and not for all businesses. Before you locate in one, take the time to find out what all the terms of occupancy are. What does your rent cover? Are there additional or hidden charges for shared facilities or services, such as parking, landscaping, decorations and signs, walkways, public rest areas, special programs, and joint advertising? What restrictions will you need to abide by? Would your business have to be open during specific hours on certain days? How much value would you really be getting for your money? Is the square footage adequate for your needs? Would your assigned space be in a good location in relationship to the surrounding businesses as well as to the flow of customer foot traffic through the shopping center or mall? Would your business be off by itself at the end of a side corridor, where customers would be likely to pass by without even noticing it?

Some other things to be aware of in evaluating a shopping center are the caliber of management operating it, the mix of businesses represented (Are they compatible or competitive? What quality of goods or services do they offer?), the number of magnet stores (department stores), which draw customers to the center, and the vacancy rate.

Locating your business in a shopping center or mall is expensive, and the various costs associated with such a location might be prohibitive for a new business owner. Furthermore, not all businesses derive any real advantage from a shopping center location. Shoe repair shops and cleaners, which provide essential services, probably would do as well, maybe even better, on a major street where their expenses would be less. The businesses that most benefit from a shopping center or mall location are the ones that cater not only to working people but to nonworking adults and to teenagers. Among these are department stores, clothing and shoe stores, record stores, book stores, gift stores, restaurants, snack stands, ice cream parlors, candy stores, and toy stores.

A major street. Major streets have the heaviest flow of automobile traffic. Though perfect for fast food restaurants, shoe repair shops, cleaners, and other stop-and-shop businesses, heavily trafficked streets can have drawbacks. Getting people to stop is one of them. If your business will be dependent on foot traffic or window shoppers, scouting a location will require more than just counting the cars passing by. What is your assessment of the array of businesses located there (antique shops or auto repair shops?), the desirability of the neighborhood, and the availability of parking?

Does the street have a character that will make your potential customers feel at ease there?

If you've decided that locating on a major street is the way to go for your business and you've found the right street, the selection process still isn't over. Which *side* of the street is best? According to market experts, the going-home side of the street is better. Because people do their shopping on their way home from work rather than on their way to work, businesses on the going-home side of the street tend to have bigger sales. Furthermore, when given a choice of shopping in sun or shade, shoppers generally choose shade. This means that businesses on the shady side of the street also have bigger sales. If the going-home side and the shady side do not coincide, you might compensate for a lack of shade by erecting an awning.

A side street. Side streets are out of the way and less frequently traveled. They may intersect or run parallel to a main street, but for one reason or another the traffic flow is less there. The main advantage of locating on a side street is lower rent. However, you also have lower visibility, which makes it difficult to attract potential customers.

For a retail business to succeed on a side street, it must be able to draw customers to it on the basis of its reputation. Sometimes this can be accomplished through word-of-mouth or advertising. The businesses most likely to prosper on a side street are seamstress and tailor shops, nursery schools, industrial suppliers, small manufacturers, and others that aren't dependent on a high traffic flow for sales.

Near a highway access. The businesses most likely to benefit from locations near highways are those that cater to the driving public by providing food, lodging, and automobile servicing. Amusements and tourist attractions also thrive on the steady flow of automobile traffic. To make the most of this location, your business must be visible from the highway and easily reached by access ramps. Travelers don't as a rule want to stray far from the highway to find you. However, a less visible location can sometimes be improved by means of a large sign that draws attention to your establishment or by means of billboard advertising that includes directions ("Take Frontage Road exit 2 blocks west").

An industrial/commercial park. In recent years the number of industrial/commercial parks being built has continued to increase. These sites are designed and built exclusively for businesses that engage in "business-to-business" selling or in industrial sales. Located on the outskirts of cities or in the suburbs where large parcels of land are available, these "parks" are often chosen by businesses for their headquarters or manufacturing operations. Among the advantages of this type of location are space, parking, desirable zoning laws, and attractive leasing rates. Since most industrial/commercial parks are off the beaten track, though, retail and service businesses that cater to the general public should normally avoid them, opting for more visible locations.

A business incubator. Business incubators are specially designed facilities for new or fledgling businesses. Created to provide enterpreneurs with affordable space and a support system (reception/secretarial services, computers, fax, duplicating equipment, and so on), incubators provide a nurturing environment in which to grow a business. Protecting new businesses at the time when they are most vulnerable, incubators often sponsor workshops and seminars for their entrepreneur tenants on such subjects as financing, marketing, and management. For more information on incubators, contact the National Business Incubation Association, One President Street, Athens, Ohio 45701.

MAKING A TRAFFIC COUNT

One way to gauge the potential sales volume of a site is to do a traffic count. This involves more than simply counting each car or person passing by. It requires that you *analyze* the flow of passers-by to determine which are *your* customers. For instance, if you're planning to operate a women's health club, you're not interested in counting the number of men who walk or drive by. Furthermore, if this club is to be very expensive, you can also rule out women who obviously would not be able to afford membership. The accuracy of your traffic count depends on your ability to assess who your potential customers are. So, prior to doing the count, you'll want to spend some time drawing up a profile of your customers to help you recognize them when they pass by.

Having determined whom to count, the next thing to do is decide the *scope* of the count. Will it encompass just the area directly in front of your store, or will it include nearby or cross traffic? Are you going to count people as they enter the area or as they leave it? If you count them at both times, there's a good chance you will be counting some people *twice*. To guard against double counting, it's essential that you set up strategic check points where your count is to be conducted.

The *timing* of your count must also be carefully planned to coincide with a normal or typical period. If you conduct your count during a peak holiday like Christmas or Easter vacation, it will be too high. Counting on Fridays or on the first day of the month could throw your tally out of balance, too, since these are the times when many people receive paychecks and social security checks.

After you've chosen the time for your count, the final step is to divide the day into half-hour intervals. In this way, you can get both a total count of the day's traffic flow and subtotals for the flows at various intervals during the day. These subtotals will tell you when to expect the heaviest sales each day, which should help you plan your hours of operation. For additional information, many business owners find it helpful to do more than one traffic count and compare the data for the various days.

RATING THE SITE

You should find it easier to determine a site's desirability if you set up a rating system of some kind, against which each site can be judged. The following score sheet shown is one example. Depending on the specific needs of your business, you may wish to modify it.

Characteristics	Grade			
	Excellent	Good	Fair	Poor
1. Centrally located to reach my market				
2. Merchandise/raw materials availability				
3. Nearby competition				
4. Transportation availability and rates				
5. Parking facilities				
6. Adequacy of utilities (sewer, water, gas, electricity)				
7. Traffic flow				
8. Taxation burden				
9. Quality of police and fire protection				
10. Environmental factors (schools, cultural and community activities)				
11. Quantity of available employees				
12. Prevailing rates of employee pay				
13. Housing availability for workers and management				
14. Local business climate				
15. Conditions of neighboring buildings				
16. Own personal feelings about area				

4

Your Building

Whether you plan to lease an existing building or construct a new one, care should be taken to ensure that the building is appropriate for your specific business. The building you finally decide on should be expected to do more than just keep the rain out. It should also promote your business and help it to function properly. Call these elements "looks" and "livability" if you will. Does the building have the looks to get a second glance from your potential customers and, better yet, to make them want to come inside? As for livability, how suitable is the building for your various business activities—selling, manufacturing, administration, shipping, receiving, storage? Unless your building gets a passing rating in both looks and livability, you're in for problems—the most common ones being lost sales, operations headaches, and remodeling costs.

LOOKS

Forget what you've heard about not judging a book by its cover. Right or wrong, this is precisely what people do every time they pass a building. Even those who never come inside and know next to nothing about your business will form opinions about it on the basis of its outside appearance—its looks alone. As such, the exterior of your building should be thought of as a communications medium, capable of transmitting messages about your business. However, if you aren't careful, it's easy to transmit the wrong message. For instance, it would be a mistake for a store selling discount housewares and appliances to be in a building with a polished marble front and brass handles. Potential customers would take one look at the marble and brass and automatically assume that the store had high prices. A brick or stucco exterior, on the other hand, would get a positive reaction, encouraging people to associate the store with economy and practicality.

Retailing

Nowhere do looks exert a greater influence on the success or failure of a business than they do in retailing. Not only must your store's exterior accurately identify the nature of your business—an exclusive shop, for example—but it must also be inviting enough to draw people inside. Achieving both ends—identification and invitation—requires planning and attention to detail. For best results, your store's architectural style, building materials, exterior colors, display windows, and signs should all be part of a coordinated effort. Ideally, each element complements the others and serves to reinforce your store's overall image. More than money, what's needed here is imagination and a clear idea of the kind of store you want to be. Once you know that, it's easier to communicate the right message to others.

Manufacturing

Manufacturing establishments have a little more room for error in the looks department than do retailers. This is because they are less dependent on their ability to draw customers inside their places of business. Customers generally don't see the plants of the companies they do business with. Orders are usually placed through wholesalers and sales representatives or by mail. Potential customers who do visit a plant are generally more interested in examining the production facilities than in admiring the building. Although the looks of your building take a back seat to its livability, this isn't to say that looks should be ignored. The exterior of your building makes a statement about the quality of the products you sell, your company's policies, and the level of success it's achieved. A rundown, unattractive building can only reflect badly on your business.

Services

Depending on the service you offer, the importance of looks can vary. Some services are so specialized that their clients actually seek them out and go to some trouble to find them (consultants, automobile repair shops, cooking schools, landscape artists). Others, such as shoe repair shops and cleaners, are frequented so regularly that customers hurry in and out, barely even noticing how the facilities look. These places don't have to use looks to pull customers in because they are coming in already. But not all services find it this easy to attract customers. Restaurants and hotels, for instance, rely a great deal on drop-in customer traffic. The more inviting their buildings are, the better it is for business.

LIVABILITY

Just because a building is deemed to comform to the local building codes doesn't make it suitable for any and all businesses. The difference between a livable building and one that's impossible depends on what you intend to do with it. The same building that's a dream come true for an automobile repair shop would probably be a nightmare for a jewelry shop. The best way to avoid selling into the wrong building is to consider the building in terms of its construction, space, design, and accessibility.

Is the building's *construction* such that it will be both safe and serviceable for your business? A manufacturer, utilizing heavy equipment, needs a building constructed of materials that can hold up to heavy wear, reduce noise, and resist fire. Cement and steel win out over wood and glass.

Does the building provide too much *space* or too little? Is there room for expansion later, should the need arise? For optimum operating efficiency, it's important to strike a balance between your present and future needs for space.

Can effective use be made of the building's *design*? This requires that the relationship between the building's selling, work, and storage areas be compatible with your business activities.

Is the building readily *accessible* to both your customers and delivery personnel? Steps, entrances (their number and location), and loading facilities all play an important role in your day-to-day operating efficiency.

LAYOUT

Layout refers to the physical set-up of furniture and fixtures, equipment, merchandise, and supplies within your building. The better your layout, the easier it is for workers to do their jobs and for customers to shop. Conversely, a bad layout can be the cause of inefficiency and lost sales.

Arriving at the right layout involves more than just moving things around and hoping for the best. It involves arranging them in a way calculated to derive the maximum benefit from the space available. The objective is to display merchandise and services to their best advantage, conserve time and motion, and fully utilize equipment. For retail businesses this translated into increased customer traffic and sales. For manufacturing and service businesses, this means increased productivity sales.

Retailing

In retailing, the main function of your layout is to direct the flow of customer traffic throughout your store. This is a two-stage process, first drawing customers into your store and then guiding them from one location to the next within it. Rather than having customers wander haphazardly, or even turn around and walk back outside, an effective layout leads customers where *you* want them to go. En route, exposure to your merchandise increases the number of purchases made. It sounds easy. And it is, if you apply a few tested principles.

1. Study your customers' shopping habits. Find out which items customers purchase regularly and which ones only occasionally. Your observations should also help you differentiate between impulse items and demand items. Impulse items are purchased on the spur of the moment, without any planning. Demand items are purchased deliberately, according to plan.

Once you know how your customers shop, you can arrange your merchandise accordingly. Take a grocery store, for instance. Where are the meat, dairy, and produce items usually located? At the back of the store or along the side walls, running from front to back. This gets customers to walk deep into the store, in order to reach them. Since these are demand items, customers don't mind the inconvenience. What's more, because these are regular purchases, customers can be counted on to seek them out repeatedly. This isn't true of such items as candy, potato chips, and magazines. As impulse items, they have to be seen to sell. Unless they are in highly visible locations—next to the checkout counter, for example—their sales will drop.

2. Create visually appealing merchandise displays. Unless your displays have eye appeal, customers will ignore them. How important is this? According to a group of independent retailers surveyed by the National Retail Merchants Association, one out of every four sales can be attributed to merchandise display. Other stores have credited displays for as much as 50 percent of their sales.

To improve your displays, notice the displays in other stores, read trade magazines, and ask your merchandise suppliers for tips. Many manufacturers will provide retailers with ready-made displays of their product at little or no charge.

3. Keep merchandise displays fresh. Even the most dramatic display starts to look commonplace when it's been left up too long. Don't let yours become permanent fixtures.

4. Coordinate merchandise displays. Merchandise that goes together should be displayed together. In this way customers are stimulated to purchase more than a single item. A customer purchasing a man's shirt is likely to buy neckties to go with it. Displaying sun glasses, suntan oil, and beach towels together is a good way to increase the sale of all three items.

5. Create a pleasant shopping environment. Make your store an enjoyable place in which to shop. In addition to being clean and attractive, it should have appropriate lighting and adequate temperature controls and ventilation. Conveniently located drinking fountains and rest rooms are also a plus.

6. Utilize space according to its value. Space directly in the path of customer traffic has the greatest sales potential and therefore the greatest value. The most valuable space of all is directly in the front of the store where customer traffic is the heaviest. The space having the least value is farthest from the traffic flow, generally in the back of the store.

Given these differences in value, it's advisable to differentiate between your selling and nonselling activities and allocate your least valuable space to nonselling activities (administration, shipping and receiving, storage, and customer service). This allows more valuable space to be utilized to generate sales. In so doing, impulse items should be located as close to the traffic flow as possible (preferably at the front of the store), and demand goods can be located farther away, in space having less value.

Manufacturing

In a manufacturing establishment the main function of your layout is to increase productivity. Whereas in retailing a layout directs the flow of customer traffic throughout the store, here it directs the flow of raw materials throughout the production process. An effective layout provides for the most efficient utilization of personnel and equipment with minimal unnecessary movement of materials.

The two most commonly used are the product layout and the process layout. A company that produces a steady flow of standardized products, such as a manufacturer of machine parts, would use a *product layout*. Here equipment is arranged in an assembly line format that corresponds to the sequence of production steps for each product. Raw materials are then located at the points where they are needed and added to the line as the unfinished products pass by. A company (such as a clothing manufacturer) whose products are non-standardized or produced in varying quantities, according to customer orders is unable to operate this way. Instead, it would use a *process layout*. Here separate processing departments are maintained and each product passes through only those processing stages it requires. Unlike the product layout, this involves additional movement of unfinished goods and leaves some equipment idle, while other equipment struggles to function beyond capacity. These problems can be partially remedied through efficient scheduling and by keeping a close watch on production activities to streamline them wherever possible.

Services

Service establishments fit into two categories: those oriented toward merchandising (beauty salons, restaurants, hotels) and those oriented toward processing (automobile repair shops, cleaners, plumbers). Layouts for merchandise-oriented businesses normally are similar to those of retail operations, whereas processing services tend to follow manufacturing layouts. The reason for these differences stems from their respective goals: to increase customer traffic or to increase productivity.

RATING YOUR BUILDING

The following Building Evaluation Sheet can help you to get a better idea of a building's ability to meet the specific needs of your business. This can be useful both in selecting the building in which you want to locate and in designing your layout for optimum efficiency.

BUILDING EVALUATION SHEET

Characteristics	Grade			
	Excellent	Good	Fair	Poor
1. Physical suitability of building				
2. Type and cost of lease				
3. Overall estimate of quality of site in 10 years				
4. Provision for future expansion				
5. History of building				
6. Exterior of building in promoting your business				
7. A safe environment for customers and employees				
8. Conformity to all zoning requirements				
9. Ready accessibility for customers				
10. Effectiveness of merchandise displays				
11. Pleasantness as place to shop				
12. Quality of lighting				
13. Utilization of space according to its value				
14. Layout in facilitating movement of employees and materials				

5

Structuring the Business

The type of legal form that you select for your new business can be crucial in determining its success. Your ability to make decisions rapidly, compete in the marketplace, and raise additional capital when needed is directly related to the legal structure of your business.

There are three legal forms to choose from: sole proprietorship, partnership, and corporation. No one form is better than another. Each has its advantages and disadvantages. The important thing is to ascertain the legal form of business that will work best for you.

Some questions you should ask yourself:

- What do I already know about this type of business?
- In what areas of the business will I need help?
- How much money will I need to get started?
- What sources of money will be available to me later?
- What kinds of risks will I be exposed to?
- How can I limit my liability?
- What kinds of taxes will I be expected to pay?

SOLE PROPRIETORSHIP

More than 75 percent of all businesses in the United States today are sole proprietorships. This means that they are owned by just one person. And, more often than not, that person is directly involved in the day-to-day operation of the business.

As a sole proprietor, you're in the driver's seat. In addition to having total control over your business, you have total responsibility for it. Just as all profits from its operation will be yours, so will all its debts and liabilities be yours as well.

Advantages of a Sole Proprietorship

You're the boss.   As a sole proprietor, you have the freedom to run your business in any legal way you choose. You can expand or contract your business, add or drop products or services, and hire, promote, and fire personnel. This ability to make decisions quickly, without having to wait for committee approval, lets you take advantage of timely opportunities. If you are looking for maximum control and minimum government interference, the sole proprietorship could be just the thing.

It's easy to get started.   The sole proprietorship is by far the simplest legal form you can choose. There's no legal expense or red tape in getting started. All you need to do is obtain the assets and commence operations. In some instances, local or state licenses may be required, such as if food or beverages are to be sold. But more often it's just a matter of hanging up your shingle.

You keep all profits.   All profits from a sole proprietorship go to the owner. You are not obligated to share them with anyone else. It's up to you whether to keep them for your personal use or reinvest them in the business.

Income from the business is taxed as personal income.   The government considers income derived from a sole proprietorship to be part of the owner's income. As such, you will have no separate income tax to pay. Furthermore, losses incurred by the business can be deducted from your personal income tax.

You can discontinue your business at will.   Should you decide you want to go on to something new, dissolving your business is quite simple. Without the necessity to get second opinions, divide up shares, or process paperwork, you need only cease operations.

Disadvantages of a Sole Proprietorship

You assume unlimited liability. A sole proprietor is responsible for all business debts or legal judgments against the business. In the event that these exceed the assets of the business, your own personal assets—home, automobile, savings account, investments—can be claimed by creditors. In other words, your financial liability is not limited to the amount of your investment in your business, but extends to your total ability to make payment. This unlimited liability is the sole proprietorship's worst feature. (Methods for protecting yourself are discussed in Chapter 15.)

The investment capital you can raise is limited. The amount of investment capital available to your business is limited to the money you have or are able to borrow. Unlike partnerships or corporations, which can draw on the resources of others, sole proprietors have to provide the total investment for their businesses.

You need to be a generalist. Anyone who starts a sole proprietorship must be prepared to perform a variety of functions, ranging from accounting to advertising. Most new sole proprietorships can't afford the luxury of hiring specialists for these tasks. Even if you can, you have to understand what they're doing, since you're the one who will be held liable for their actions.

Retaining high-caliber employees is difficult. You may have difficulty in holding onto your best employees because they want more than you are offering them—namely, part ownership in your business. For these employees a good salary and bonuses usually won't be enough. Your only recourse is to let them go or to convert your sole proprietorship to a partnership.

The life of the business is limited. The death of the owner automatically terminates a sole proprietorship, as does any other unforeseen occurrence (long-term illness, for example) that keeps the owner from operating the business. Since there is no one else to carry on, the business just ceases to function.

PARTNERSHIP

A partnership exists when two or more people share in the ownership of a business. By agreement, they determine the amount of time and money each partner will invest in the business and the percentage of the profits that each will receive. The extent of each partner's authority and liability must also be made clear.

To avoid misunderstandings later, everything that has been agreed to should be put in writing, preferably with the assistance of an attorney. The importance of a written partnership agreement cannot be overemphasized. In the absence of such a document, the courts can resolve any disputes that arise, but the outcome might not be to your liking.

Here is some of the information that should be included in your partnership agreement:

- Each partner's responsibilities and authority.
- The extent of each partner's liability.
- The amount of capital each partner is investing in the business.
- How profits and losses are to be shared.
- How disputes between the partners are to be resolved.
- Arrangements for the withdrawal or admission of partners.
- How assets are to be distributed should the business be dissolved.

Advantages of a Partnership

Two heads are better than one. In a partnership you have the advantage of being able to draw on the skills and abilities of each partner. Ideally, the contributions that each partner is able to make to the business complement those of the other partners. For instance, one partner oversees accounting functions, another is in charge of production, another handles sales.

It's easy to get started. Starting a partnership is relatively easy. Although it entails additional cost and more planning than a sole proprietorship (selecting partners, preparing the partnership agreement, and so on), red tape is minimal.

More investment capital is available. Your company's ability to increase capital can be enhanced by simply bringing in more partners. Unlike a sole proprietorship, which can draw on the financial resources of only one individual, in a partnership you have the combined resources of the partners.

Partners pay only personal income tax. Partnerships are taxed the same as a sole proprietorship. The total income of the business is considered to be the personal income of the partners. This means there is no separate business income tax to pay, and business losses are deductible from each partner's income tax.

High-caliber employees can be made partners. Partnerships are able to attract and retain high-caliber employees by offering them the opportunity to become partners. This method of employee motivation has been particularly successful in the legal and accounting professions.

Disadvantages of a Partnership

Partners have unlimited liability. Like sole proprietors, partners are responsible for all debts or legal judgments against the business. This liability is even worse for partners than it is for sole proprietors because, as a partner, you are responsible not only for your own debts but for those of your partners. Should they incur liabilities, you could be left holding the bag. And remember that, even though your investment in the business may be minimal, your losses could be substantial. Your liability extends beyond the amount of your investment to include your personal assets as well.

Profits must be shared. All profits resulting from the partnership must be distributed among the partners in accordance with the partnership agreement. What percentage of the profits is to be reinvested in the company must be decided by the partners. Your wishes in this matter represent only one viewpoint.

The partners may disagree. Disputes among partners can literally destroy a partnership. One partner's desire to expand the business can go against another partner's goal of cutting costs. Should your money be spent on improving your product or on promoting it? When key decisions must be made, the feelings of trust and admiration that drew you together as partners can disintegrate. If this is to be avoided, you must give your full attention to selecting partners and drawing up the partnership agreement. Foresight in the planning stage can pay off later.

The life of the business is limited. As with a sole proprietorship, the life of a partnership is limited. Should one of your partners withdraw from the business or die or become too ill to carry on, the partnership is automatically dissolved. Though it is possible for the remaining partners to reorganize the business, the financial interest of the departing partner must first be paid. Furthermore, any time a new partner is admitted to the business, dissolution of the partnership is mandatory. A new partnership, reflecting the addition of the new partner, must be formed.

Limited Partnerships

Because of the unlimited liability that partners are subject to, you may be reluctant to assume the risk. One way around this is to form a limited partnership. In a limited partnership there are two kinds of partners—general and limited. *General partners* assume unlimited liability for the business. The liability of *limited partners* is confined to the amounts of their investments. However, in exchange for this limited liability, limited partners are restricted from taking an active role in the company's management. And the withdrawal of a limited partner from the business does not necessarily dissolve the partnership, should others wish it to continue.

In a limited partnership the risk can be shifted from one partner to another. It cannot be avoided entirely, though, since every limited partnership must have a least one general partner. If you decide to set up a limited partnership, public notice to this effect, stating that one or more partners have limited status, must be made. Otherwise it is assumed that a general partnership exists, in which all partners have liability.

Other Partners

Within the scope of the partnership format, there are four other types of partners you may wish to consider.

1. *Silent partners* invest money in a business but take no active role in its management; nor do they share liability. They are primarily interested in getting a return on their investment.

2. *Secret partners* are active in the management of the business, but are not known to be partners. Although they want to participate in running the business, they don't want the public to know about their involvement.

3. *Dormant partners* are neither active in the business nor known to the public. Like silent partners, they are concerned with getting a return on their investment. Like secret partners, they want to maintain their privacy.

4. *Nominal partners* aren't partners at all, but by their behavior they lead the public to believe that they are. An example of this is the person who permits his name to be associated with the business in exchange for a fee.

Depending on your company's needs, one or more of these kinds of partners may be right for you.

Joint Venture

The kinds of partnership just described all share the intention of being ongoing businesses. A joint venture differs from these in that it is a partnership set up for a specific purpose of limited duration. For example, suppose you and a friend decided to buy, renovate, and resell a house together. Your joint venture would start when you purchased the house and end when you sold it. As for your taxes, joint ventures are taxed the same as partnerships.

During the life of such a joint venture, each partner is subject to unlimited liability. So the same caution should be exercised in selecting a joint venture partner as in selecting any other partner. Also, problems can be avoided by consulting an attorney and putting the terms of your joint venture agreement in writing.

CORPORATION

A corporation differs from other legal forms of business in that the law considers it to be an artificial being, possessing the same rights and responsibilities as a person. Unlike a sole proprietorship or a partnership, a corporation has an existence separate from its owners. As such, it can sue and be sued, own property, agree to contracts, and engage in business transactions. Additionally, since a corporation is a separate entity, it is not dissolved with every change in ownership. The result of this is that corporations have the potential for unlimited life.

The Corporate Charter

To form a corporation you must be granted a charter by the state in which your business resides. Each state sets its own requirements and fees for the issuance of charters. The cost for incorporating a small business usually ranges from $1,000 to $3,000. Generally, your charter must include such information as:

- Your corporation's name.
- Names of principal stockholders.
- Number and types of shares to be issued.
- Place of business.
- Type of business.

Stockholders

Each person who owns stock in your corporation is a co-owner with you in the business. This does not meant that every stockholder will actively participate in your company's management, or even be associated with it in any way, other than by purchasing shares of the corporation's stock. They are guaranteed the right to vote on the members of the corporation's board of directors and on certain major corporate policies.

Enabling people to become co-owners in a business in this way benefits both the corporation and the stockholders. The corporation is able to obtain investment capital and the stockholders can share in whatever profits the corporation earns. These profits are distributed to stockholders in the form of dividends. Furthermore, since stock is transferable, stockholders are free to sell their stock at any time and receive the current market value for it.

The Board of Directors

The board of directors represents the stockholders and is responsible for protecting their interests. Board members are elected annually, usually for one-year terms, which can be renewed indefinitely by means of the election process. Since the number of votes that stockholders can cast is related to the number of shares they have, major stockholders can virtually elect themselves to the board.

The board of directors generally concerns itself with determining corporate policies, rather than taking care of day-to-day operations. To handle these, the board appoints the chief executive officer and other top corporate officers—vice presidents, secretary, treasurer, and so on. They, in turn, see that the policies stipulated by the board of directors are implemented.

Advantages of a Corporation

Stockholders have limited liability. One of the most attractive advantages of the corporate form of business is that the owners have limited liability. Investors are financially liable only up to the amounts of their investments in the corporation. This limited liability ensures that creditors of the corporation cannot touch your personal assets.

Corporations can raise the most investment capital. You can increase the investment capital in your corporation simply by selling more shares of stock. Whereas sole proprietorships and partnerships are limited in the number of owners they can have, a corporation can have any number of owners.

Corporations have unlimited life. Because of its status as a legal entity, a corporation has its own identity. Unlike sole proprietorships and partnerships, whose lifespans are linked to those of their owners, it is possible for your corporation to exist indefinitely. The withdrawal of stockholders, corporate officers, or employees will not terminate its existence.

Ownership is easily transferable. Ownership in a corporation is easily transferable from one person to another. Investors can buy and sell shares of stock as they please without seeking the prior approval of anyone. In addition to providing investors with maximum control over their investments, this enables your corporation to go on operating without disruption.

Corporations utilize specialists. Because of the separation of ownership and management, the corporate form of business can most effectively utilize the services of specialists. Unlike sole proprietorships and partnerships, which tend to rely on the skills and abilities of the owners to perform each function, corporations employ specialists. The availability of specially trained personnel leads to higher productivity and increased efficiency.

Disadvantages of a Corporation

Corporations are taxed twice. Unlike sole proprietorships and partnerships, corporations and their owners are taxed separately. In what amounts to double taxation, both the income your corporation earns and the income you as an individual earn are taxed. This is the primary drawback to the corporate form.

THE ADVANTAGES AND DISADVANTAGES OF EACH LEGAL FORM OF OWNERSHIP

Sole Proprietorship

Advantages	Disadvantages
1. You're the boss.	1. You assume unlimited liability.
2. It's easy to get started.	2. The investment capital you can raise is limited.
3. You keep all the profits.	
4. Income from business is taxed as personal income.	3. You need to be a generalist.
	4. Retaining high-caliber employees is difficult.
5. You can discontinue your business at will.	5. The life of the business is limited.

Partnership

Advantages	Disadvantages
1. Two heads are better than one.	1. Partners have unlimited liability.
2. It's easy to get started.	2. Profits must be shared.
3. More investment capital is available.	3. The partners may disagree.
	4. The life of the business is limited.
4. Partners pay only personal income tax.	
5. High-caliber employees can be made partners.	

Corporation

Advantages	Disadvantages
1. Stockholders have limited liability.	1. Corporations are taxed twice.
	2. Corporations must pay capital stock tax.
2. Corporations can raise the most investment capital.	
	3. Starting a corporation is expensive.
3. Corporations have unlimited life.	
4. Ownership is easily transferable.	4. Corporations are more closely regulated.
5. Corporations utilize specialists.	

Corporations must pay a capital stock tax. In addition to paying a corporate federal income tax, corporations must pay a capital stock tax. This is an annual tax on outstanding shares of stock which is levied by the state in which the business is incorporated.

Starting a corporation is expensive. More expense is involved in starting a corporation than is involved in starting any other legal form of business. There are the costs for legal assistance in drawing up your charter, state incorporation fees, and the purchase of record books and stock certificates. All these require expenditures not only of money but of time.

Corporations are more closely regulated. The government regulates corporations much more closely than it does any other forms of business. Numerous state and federal reports must be filed regularly. And each year, corporations are required to prepare, print, and distribute an annual report summarizing the company's activities during the preceding year. Often specialists are retained on staff solely for the purpose of providing the data for these reports.

S Corporation

If you are interested in forming a corporation, but hesitate to do so because of the double taxation, there is a way to avoid it. You can do this by making your business an S corporation. The Internal Revenue Service permits this type of corporation to be taxed as a partnership rather than as a corporation. However, to qualify for S status, your business must meet the specific requirements set forth by the IRS. These include limits on (1) the number and type of shareholders in the business, (2) the stock that is issued, and (3) the corporation's sources of revenues. For more information on forming an S corporation, ask the IRS for its free publication, *Tax Guide for Small Business*, publication number 334.

GOVERNMENT REGULATION

Depending on what you sell and where your business is located, there will also be various permits and paperwork to take care of and trademarks, patents, and copyrights to consider.

To protect your business's legal standing in the community it's important to find out which local, state, and federal regulations apply to it.

Local Regulations

At the local level, regulations pertaining to businesses are primarily concerned with taxation, public health and safety, and zoning. Although each community is different, the most typical forms of regulation are:

- Business taxes and permits.
- Fictitious business name statements.
- Zoning restrictions.
- Other regulations.

Business taxes and permits. Commonly referred to as a *business license*, a permit is issued by the city and/or county in which a business is located and is usually valid for one to two years. The fee for it, which is based on the gross sales of your business, can range from less than $50 to more than $250. To find out if a business license is necessary in your particular circumstances and/or which agency issues it, check the *White Pages* of your telephone directory under City of — — —, Business Tax Division, Business Licenses, or City Clerk.

Fictitious business name statement. If you're planning to operate your business under a name other than your own, such as B&G Enterprises or Midtown Realty Company, then you'll probably need to file a fictitious business name statement with the county clerk's office. The purpose of this statement is to inform the public of your identity and the identities of any others who are co-owners in the business.

Providing this public notice is a two-part process that involves (1) filing the statement with the county clerk, and (2) having the statement published in a newspaper of general circulation. You can usually eliminate the first part, though, by going directly to the newspaper that's going to run your statement. As a convenience to their customers, most newspapers keep fictitious business name forms on hand (see page 53) and will file the completed statement for you. The total cost for filing and publishing the statement should be somewhere between $30 and $90.

Zoning restrictions. Just as some people are more entrepreneurially inclined than others, so are some communities. Whereas one city may encourage businesses to locate there, another may not.

FICTITIOUS BUSINESS NAME STATEMENT

REMINDER
1. Submit original and 3 copies.
2. Filing fee $24.00 for one business name.
   $5.00 for each additional business name.
   $5.00 for each additional partner after first two.
3. **Provide return stamped envelope if mailed.**

☐ New Fictitious Business
    Name Statement

☐ Refile

GARY L. GRANVILLE, COUNTY CLERK
PUBLIC SERVICES DIVISION
211 W. SANTA ANA BOULEVARD
POST OFFICE BOX 22013
SANTA ANA, CA 92702-2013

THIS STATEMENT WAS FILED WITH THE COUNTY CLERK OF ORANGE COUNTY ON DATE INDICATED BY FILE STAMP BELOW.

FICTITIOUS BUSINESS NAME STATEMENT

File No. _____   THE FOLLOWING PERSON(S) IS (ARE) DOING BUSINESS AS: (TYPE ALL INFORMATION)

1.	Fictitious Business Name(s)
2.	Street Address, City & State of Principal place of Business in California Zip Code
3.	Full name of Registrant (if corporation—show state of incorporation)
	Residence Address City State Zip Code
	Full name of Registrant (if corporation—show state of incorporation)
	Residence Address City State Zip Code
	Full name of Registrant (if corporation—show state of incorporation)
	Residence Address City State Zip Code

4. (CHECK ONE ONLY) This business is conducted by ( ) an individual ( ) a general partnership ( ) a limited partnership ( ) an unincorporated association other than a partnership ( ) a corporation ( ) a business trust ( ) co-partners ( ) husband and wife ( ) joint venture ( ) other—please specify)

5. THE REGISTRANT(S) COMMENCED TO TRANSACT BUSINESS UNDER THE FICTITIOUS BUSINESS NAME(S) LISTED ABOVE ON:

DATE:

NOTICE: THIS FICTITIOUS NAME STATEMENT EXPIRES FIVE YEARS FROM THE DATE IT WAS FILED IN THE OFFICE OF THE COUNTY CLERK. A NEW FICTITIOUS BUSINESS NAME STATEMENT MUST BE FILED BEFORE THAT TIME. THE FILING OF THIS STATEMENT DOES NOT OF ITSELF AUTHORIZE THE USE IN THIS STATE OF A FICTITIOUS BUSINESS NAME IN VIOLATION OF THE RIGHTS OF ANOTHER UNDER FEDERAL, STATE, OR COMMON LAW (SEE SECTION 14400 ET SEQ., BUSINESS AND PROFESSIONS CODE).

6. Signature _____

     (TYPE OR PRINT NAME)

If Registrant is a corporation sign below:

Corporation Name _____

Signature & Title _____

FILE NO _____

FO182-266.13 (7/92)   FILE WITH COUNTY CLERK

Typically regulated things include the types of businesses that are acceptable, the size and placement of signs, exterior merchandise displays, inventory storage, parking, and hours of operation. Since the main purpose of zoning restrictions is to protect the rights of people and property, a business that is noisy, smelly, or unsightly can expect to run into trouble. To find out the zoning restrictions for your community, contact your local planning department.

Other regulations. Depending on the nature of your business, other local regulations may also apply. For instance, if you are engaged in food preparation, processing, or serving (mail order cheesecakes, pizza restaurant, catering), you must stay within the county health department codes. Antique dealers often find that a permit from the police department is a prerequisite for doing business because stolen goods are sometimes sold through dealers. Other departments that have jurisdiction over businesses include the fire and sanitation departments.

State Regulations

At the state level, regulations pertaining to businesses center around taxation and the monitoring of specific professions. Each state sets its own standards in these areas, but the most common regulations involve the issuing of seller's permits and occupational licenses.

Seller's permit. Many states require anyone who buys and sells merchandise to obtain a seller's permit. This permit (1) exempts you from paying sales tax on the merchandise you purchase for resale through your business, and (2) authorizes you to collect sales tax from your customers.

Usually there is no fee to obtain a seller's permit, but, depending on your estimated gross sales for the year, you may be required to post a bond. This is to ensure that you collect and remit to the state all sales tax due. To find out more about the seller's permit and whether or not you should have one, check your telephone directory *White Pages* under "State of — — — Taxes."

*Occupational license.*To maintain set standards of performance and protect the safety of consumers, most states regulate entry into specific occupations or professions, such as those in the health services, cosmetology, accounting, and real estate fields. If your business is in a regulated field, you must first meet the standards set forth by the state licensing board governing your occupation. Once you have demonstrated your competence, you will be issued a license, which is usually valid for a period of one to two years and is renewable. To determine if an occupational license is required for your business activity, check with your state's Department of Consumer Affairs.

Federal Regulations

At the federal level, regulations pertaining to businesses focus on taxation, employer responsibilities, consumer protection, and the registration of trademarks, patents, and copyrights.

Employer identification number. If you employ one or more persons in your business, the federal government requires you to have an employer identification number. This enables the government to verify that you are paying all appropriate employer taxes and withholding the proper amounts from employee paychecks. Even though you may not have any employees in the beginning, it's still advisable to obtain a number, especially if you sell to businesses, because customers often need it for their records. And if you should decide to hire someone later, take in a partner, or incorporate, you will need the number for tax purposes. Obtaining your identification number is an easy matter. What's more, there is no fee for it. Just fill out IRS form number SS-4 (shown on page 56) and submit it to the Internal Revenue Service.

Consumer protection regulation. To protect the rights of consumers, the federal government regulates business practices in a variety of areas. Businesses that engage in mail order sales or sell their products in more than one state are subject to regulation by the Federal Trade Commission, Interstate Commerce Commission, and/or the U.S. Postal Service. The Federal Trade Commission also oversees product packaging and labeling, product warranties, and advertising claims. With nutritional supplements, health care products, or cosmetics, the Food and Drug Administration steps into the picture. Financial services businesses may come under the jurisdiction of the Securities and Exchange Commission. To familiarize yourself with the regulations that apply to your type of business, write to the Federal Trade Commission, Washington, D.C. 20580.

Trademarks, patents, and copyrights. In addition to protecting the rights of consumers, the federal government also protects the

Form **SS-4** (Rev. April 1991) Department of the Treasury Internal Revenue Service	**Application for Employer Identification·Number** (For use by employers and others. Please read the attached instructions before completing this form.)	EIN OMB No. 1545-0003 Expires 4-30-94

Please type or print clearly.

1 Name of applicant (True legal name) (See instructions.)

2 Trade name of business, if different from name in line 1 | **3** Executor, trustee, "care of" name

4a Mailing address (street address) (room, apt., or suite no.) | **5a** Address of business (See instructions.)

4b City, state, and ZIP code | **5b** City, state, and ZIP code

6 County and state where principal business is located

7 Name of principal officer, grantor, or general partner (See instructions.) ▶

8a Type of entity (Check only one box.) (See instructions.)
- ☐ Individual SSN _____
- ☐ REMIC   ☐ Personal service corp.
- ☐ State/local government   ☐ National guard
- ☐ Other nonprofit organization (specify) _____
- ☐ Other (specify) ▶ _____
- ☐ Estate
- ☐ Plan administrator SSN _____
- ☐ Other corporation (specify) _____
- ☐ Federal government/military   ☐ Church or church controlled organization
- If nonprofit organization enter GEN (if applicable) _____
- ☐ Trust
- ☐ Partnership
- ☐ Farmers' cooperative

8b If a corporation, give name of foreign country (if applicable) or state in the U.S. where incorporated ▶ | Foreign country | State

9 Reason for applying (Check only one box.)
- ☐ Started new business
- ☐ Hired employees
- ☐ Created a pension plan (specify type) ▶ _____
- ☐ Banking purpose (specify) ▶
- ☐ Changed type of organization (specify) ▶ _____
- ☐ Purchased going business
- ☐ Created a trust (specify) ▶ _____
- ☐ Other (specify) ▶

10 Date business started or acquired (Mo., day, year) (See instructions.) | **11** Enter closing month of accounting year. (See instructions.)

12 First date wages or annuities were paid or will be paid (Mo., day, year). **Note:** *If applicant is a withholding agent, enter date income will first be paid to nonresident alien. (Mo., day, year)* . . . . ▶

13 Enter highest number of employees expected in the next 12 months. **Note:** *If the applicant does not expect to have any employees during the period, enter "0."* . . . . ▶ | Nonagricultural | Agricultural | Household

14 Principal activity (See instructions.) ▶

15 Is the principal business activity manufacturing? . . . . ☐ **Yes**   ☐ **No**
If "Yes," principal product and raw material used ▶

16 To whom are most of the products or services sold? Please check the appropriate box.   ☐ Business (wholesale)
☐ Public (retail)   ☐ Other (specify) ▶ _____   ☐ N/A

17a Has the applicant ever applied for an identification number for this or any other business? . . . . ☐ **Yes**   ☐ **No**
Note: *If "Yes," please complete lines 17b and 17c.*

17b If you checked the "Yes" box in line 17a, give applicant's true name and trade name, if different than name shown on prior application.

True name ▶ | Trade name ▶

17c Enter approximate date, city, and state where the application was filed and the previous employer identification number if known.

Approximate date when filed (Mo., day, year)	City and state where filed	Previous EIN

Under penalties of perjury, I declare that I have examined this application, and to the best of my knowledge and belief, it is true, correct, and complete | Telephone number (include area code)

Name and title (Please type or print clearly.) ▶

Signature ▶ | Date ▶

Note: *Do not write below this line.   For official use only.*

Please leave blank ▶	Geo.	Ind.	Class	Size	Reason for applying

For Paperwork Reduction Act Notice, see attached instructions. | Cat. No. 16055N | Form **SS-4** (Rev. 4-91)

rights of entrepreneurs. In this case it protects your right to use and profit from your own name (or business or product name), inventions, and artistic creations.

The following information should give you a better idea of the protection provided by trademarks, patents, and copyrights, as well as how you can use them to your advantage.

- Trademarks. By definition, a *trademark* is any word, name, symbol, device, or combination of these used to identify the products or services of a business and to distinguish them from those of other enterprises. Often one of a business's most valuable assets, a trademark can help to define its image, increase customer awareness, and stimulate repeat purchases. Although a business isn't required by law to register its trademark, this is advisable since it offers the greatest protection (see application form on pages 58 and 59. Once a trademark is registered, the holder's right to use it extends for a period of ten years, at which time registration is renewable. For more information on trademarks, write the U.S. Department of Commerce, Patent and Trademark Office, Washington, D.C. 20231, and ask them to send you their pamphlet, "General Information Concerning Trademarks."

- Patents. In granting a *patent* to a business, the federal government gives it the right to exclude all others from making, using, or selling the invention in the United States. Patents for new and useful products or processes are valid for 17 years. A design patent, covering only the style or appearance of a product, may be valid for a period ranging from $3^{1/2}$ to 14 years.

  If you develop a product, process, or design you believe has commercial possibilities, obtaining a patent may be advisable, given the protection it affords. The government recommends that inventors not attempt to prepare their own patent applications without the help of a registered attorney or agent skilled in patent procedures. Taking this into consideration, when legal fees are added in, the total cost of obtaining a patent runs between $2,000 and $5,000.

  To get the basic facts on obtaining a patent, read "Patents and Inventions: An Information Aid for Inventors," published by the U.S. Department of Commerce, Patent and Trademark Office, Washington, D.C. 20231.

- Copyrights. A *copyright* protects the right of an individual to keep others from copying his or her creations. Although most commonly associated with literary works, copyright protection extends to

TRADEMARK APPLICATION (FRONT)

| TRADEMARK APPLICATION, PRINCIPAL REGISTER, WITH DECLARATION (Partnership) | **MARK** *(identify the mark)* |
| | **CLASS NO.** *(if known)* |

TO THE COMMISSIONER OF PATENTS AND TRADEMARKS:

NAME OF PARTNERSHIP

NAMES OF PARTNERS

BUSINESS ADDRESS OF PARTNERSHIP

CITIZENSHIP OF PARTNERS

The above identified applicant has adopted and is using the trademark shown in the accompanying drawing[1] for the following goods: _____

_____

and requests that said mark be registered in the United States Patent and Trademark Office on the Principal Register established by the Act of July 5, 1946.

The trademark was first used on the goods[2] on _____ ; was first used on the goods[2] in
                (date)
_____ commerce[3] on _____ ; and is now in use in
   (type of commerce)   *(date)*
such commerce.

4

The mark is used by applying it to[5] _____

_____

and five specimens showing the mark as actually used are presented herewith.

6

_____
                                  (name of partner)
being hereby warned that willful false statements and the like so made are punishable by fine or imprisonment, or both, under Section 1001 of Title 18 of the United States Code and that such willful false statements may jeopardize the validity of the application or any registration resulting therefrom, declares that he/she is a partner of applicant partnership; he/she believes said partnership to be the owner of the trademark sought to be registered; to the best of his/her knowledge and belief no other person, firm, corporation, or association has the right to use said mark in commerce, either in the identical form or in such near resemblance thereto as may be likely, when applied to the goods of such other person, to cause confusion, or to cause mistake, or to deceive; the facts set forth in this application are true; and all statements made of his/her own knowledge are true and all statements made on information and belief are believed to be true.

_____
                            (signature of partner)

_____
                            (date)

Form PTO - 1477 (4 - 82)   *(Instructions on reverse side)*   Patent and Trademark Office - U.S. DEPT. of COMMERCE
(over)

58

TRADEMARK APPLICATION (BACK)

REPRESENTATION

If the applicant is not domiciled in the United States, a domestic representative must be designated. See Form 4.4.

If applicant wishes to furnish a power of attorney, see Form 4.2. An attorney at law is not required to furnish a power.

FOOTNOTES

1   If registration is sought for a word or numeral mark not depicted in any special form, the drawing may be the mark typed in capital letters on letter-size bond paper; otherwise, the drawing should be made with india ink on a good grade of bond paper or on bristol board.

2   If more than one item of goods in a class is set forth and the dates given for that class apply to only one of the items listed, insert the name of the item to which the dates apply.

3   Type of commerce should be specified as "interstate," "territorial," "foreign," or other type of commerce which may lawfully be regulated by Congress. Foreign applicants relying upon use must specify commerce which Congress may regulate, using wording such as commerce with the United States or commerce between the United States and a foreign country.

4   If the mark is other than a coined, arbitrary or fanciful mark, and the mark is believed to have acquired a secondary meaning, insert whichever of the following paragraphs is applicable:

   a) The mark has become distinctive of applicant's goods as a result of substantially exclusive and continuous use in _____ commerce for the five years next preceding the date of filing
   (type of commerce)
   of this application.

   b) The mark has become distinctive of applicant's goods as evidenced by the showing submitted separately.

5   Insert the manner or method of using the mark with the goods, i.e., "the goods," "the containers for the goods," "displays associated with the goods," "tags or labels affixed to the goods," or other method which may be in use.

6   The required fee of $175.00 for each class must be submitted. (An application to register the same mark for goods and/or services in more than one class may be filed; however, goods and/or services and dates of use, by class, must be set out separately, and specimens and a fee for each class are required.)

FORM TX

UNITED STATES COPYRIGHT OFFICE

REGISTRATION NUMBER

TX   TXU

EFFECTIVE DATE OF REGISTRATION

Month   Day   Year

DO NOT WRITE ABOVE THIS LINE. IF YOU NEED MORE SPACE, USE A SEPARATE CONTINUATION SHEET.

1

TITLE OF THIS WORK ▼

PREVIOUS OR ALTERNATIVE TITLES ▼

PUBLICATION AS A CONTRIBUTION If this work was published as a contribution to a periodical, serial, or collection, give information about the collective work in which the contribution appeared. **Title of Collective Work ▼**

If published in a periodical or serial give: Volume ▼   Number ▼   Issue Date ▼   On Pages ▼

2

a

NAME OF AUTHOR ▼

DATES OF BIRTH AND DEATH
Year Born ▼   Year Died ▼

Was this contribution to the work a "work made for hire"?
☐ Yes
☐ No

AUTHOR'S NATIONALITY OR DOMICILE
Name of Country
OR { Citizen of ▶_____
{ Domiciled in ▶_____

WAS THIS AUTHOR'S CONTRIBUTION TO THE WORK
Anonymous? ☐ Yes ☐ No
Pseudonymous? ☐ Yes ☐ No
If the answer to either of these questions is "Yes," see detailed instructions.

NATURE OF AUTHORSHIP Briefly describe nature of the material created by this author in which copyright is claimed. ▼

NOTE

Under the law, the "author" of a "work made for hire" is generally the employer, not the employee (see instructions). For any part of this work that was "made for hire" check "Yes" in the space provided, give the employer (or other person for whom the work was prepared) as "Author" of that part, and leave the space for dates of birth and death blank.

b

NAME OF AUTHOR ▼

DATES OF BIRTH AND DEATH
Year Born ▼   Year Died ▼

Was this contribution to the work a "work made for hire"?
☐ Yes
☐ No

AUTHOR'S NATIONALITY OR DOMICILE
Name of country
OR { Citizen of ▶_____
{ Domiciled in ▶_____

WAS THIS AUTHOR'S CONTRIBUTION TO THE WORK
Anonymous? ☐ Yes ☐ No
Pseudonymous? ☐ Yes ☐ No
If the answer to either of these questions is "Yes," see detailed instructions.

NATURE OF AUTHORSHIP Briefly describe nature of the material created by this author in which copyright is claimed. ▼

c

NAME OF AUTHOR ▼

DATES OF BIRTH AND DEATH
Year Born ▼   Year Died ▼

Was this contribution to the work a "work made for hire"?
☐ Yes
☐ No

AUTHOR'S NATIONALITY OR DOMICILE
Name of Country
OR { Citizen of ▶_____
{ Domiciled in ▶_____

WAS THIS AUTHOR'S CONTRIBUTION TO THE WORK
Anonymous? ☐ Yes ☐ No
Pseudonymous? ☐ Yes ☐ No
If the answer to either of these questions is "Yes," see detailed instructions.

NATURE OF AUTHORSHIP Briefly describe nature of the material created by this author in which copyright is claimed. ▼

3

YEAR IN WHICH CREATION OF THIS WORK WAS COMPLETED This information must be given ◀ Year in all cases.

DATE AND NATION OF FIRST PUBLICATION OF THIS PARTICULAR WORK
Complete this information Month ▶_____ Day ▶_____ Year ▶_____
ONLY if this work has been published. ◀ Nation

4

COPYRIGHT CLAIMANT(S) Name and address must be given even if the claimant is the same as the author given in space 2.▼

See instructions before completing this space

APPLICATION RECEIVED

ONE DEPOSIT RECEIVED

TWO DEPOSITS RECEIVED

REMITTANCE NUMBER AND DATE

DO NOT WRITE HERE — OFFICE USE ONLY

TRANSFER If the claimant(s) named here in space 4 are different from the author(s) named in space 2, give a brief statement of how the claimant(s) obtained ownership of the copyright.▼

MORE ON BACK ▶ • Complete all applicable spaces (numbers 5-11) on the reverse side of this page.
• See detailed instructions.   • Sign the form at line 10.

DO NOT WRITE HERE

Page 1 of_____pages

COPYRIGHT APPLICATION FORM (BACK)

DO NOT WRITE ABOVE THIS LINE. IF YOU NEED MORE SPACE, USE A SEPARATE CONTINUATION SHEET.

PREVIOUS REGISTRATION Has registration for this work, or for an earlier version of this work, already been made in the Copyright Office?
☐ Yes ☐ No If your answer is "Yes," why is another registration being sought? (Check appropriate box) ▼
☐ This is the first published edition of a work previously registered in unpublished form.
☐ This is the first application submitted by this author as copyright claimant.
☐ This is a changed version of the work, as shown by space 6 on this application.
If your answer is "Yes," give: **Previous Registration Number** ▼   **Year of Registration** ▼

5

DERIVATIVE WORK OR COMPILATION Complete both space 6a & 6b for a derivative work; complete only 6b for a compilation.
a. Preexisting Material Identify any preexisting work or works that this work is based on or incorporates. ▼

b. Material Added to This Work Give a brief, general statement of the material that has been added to this work and in which copyright is claimed. ▼

6

See instructions
before completing
this space

MANUFACTURERS AND LOCATIONS If this is a published work consisting preponderantly of nondramatic literary material in English, the law may require that the copies be manufactured in the United States or Canada for full protection. If so, the names of the manufacturers who performed certain processes, and the places where these processes were performed **must** be given. See instructions for details.
Names of Manufacturers ▼   **Places of Manufacture** ▼

7

REPRODUCTION FOR USE OF BLIND OR PHYSICALLY HANDICAPPED INDIVIDUALS   A signature on this form at space 10, and a check in one of the boxes here in space 8, constitutes a non-exclusive grant of permission to the Library of Congress to reproduce and distribute solely for the blind and physically handicapped and under the conditions and limitations prescribed by the regulations of the Copyright Office: (1) copies of the work identified in space 1 of this application in Braille (or similar tactile symbols); or (2) phonorecords embodying a fixation of a reading of that work; or (3) both.

a ☐ Copies and Phonorecords   b ☐ Copies Only   c ☐ Phonorecords Only

8

See instructions.

DEPOSIT ACCOUNT If the registration fee is to be charged to a Deposit Account established in the Copyright Office, give name and number of Account.
Name ▼   **Account Number** ▼

CORRESPONDENCE Give name and address to which correspondence about this application should be sent. Name/Address/Apt/City/State/Zip ▼

Area Code & Telephone Number ▶

9

Be sure to
give your
daytime phone
◀ number

CERTIFICATION* I, the undersigned, hereby certify that I am the
Check one ▶
☐ author
☐ other copyright claimant
☐ owner of exclusive right(s)
☐ authorized agent of _____
       Name of author or other copyright claimant, or owner of exclusive right(s) ▲

of the work identified in this application and that the statements made by me in this application are correct to the best of my knowledge.

Typed or printed name and date ▼ If this is a published work, this date must be the same as or later than the date of publication given in space 3.

_____ date ▶ _____

☞ Handwritten signature (X) ▼

10

MAIL CERTIFI-CATE TO

Certificate will be mailed in window envelope

Name ▼

Number/Street/Apartment Number ▼

City/State/ZIP ▼

Have you:
• Completed all necessary spaces?
• Signed your application in space 10?
• Enclosed check or money order for $10 payable to *Register of Copyrights?*
• Enclosed your deposit material with the application and fee?

MAIL TO: Register of Copyrights, Library of Congress, Washington, D.C. 20559.

11

graphic designs, paintings, sculpture, musical compositions, sound recordings, and audiovisual works. A business doesn't have to be in the arts to benefit from this protection. A sampling of the works that come within the broad scope of copyright coverage includes brochures, catalogs and advertising copy, newsletters and books, audiocassettes and video tapes, reports, charts and technical drawings, and computer programs.

Obtaining a copyright is relatively simple. All you need to do is provide public notice of the copyright on the work itself and file an application form (as shown on pages 60 and 61). The fee is currently $20, and, once granted, the copyright is good for up to 50 years after the holder's death. For more information, or a copyright form itself, write to the Copyright Office, Library of Congress, Washington, D.C. 20559. Be sure to specify the type of work you want to copyright.

STRUCTURING THE BUSINESS CHECKLIST

To make sure that you have selected a legal form that is appropriate
for your business and are familiar with the government regulations
that apply to it, answer the questions in the Structuring the Business
Checklist.

	Answer Yes or No
1. Do you know the advantages and disadvantages of each of the following legal forms?	
Sole proprietorship	_____
Partnership	_____
Corporation	_____
2. Is it clear to you why any partnership that is formed should have a written partnership agreement?	_____
3. Do you know what information to include in a partnership agreement?	_____
4. Are you aware of the difference between a general and a limited partnership?	_____
5. Can you describe the characteristics of each of the following partners?	
Silent	_____
Secret	_____
Dormant	_____
6. Do you know what a joint venture is?	_____
7. Do you know what steps are required to incorporate your business?	_____
8. Have you considered the benefits to be derived from forming an S corporation?	_____
9. Are you aware of the local, state, and federal regulations that apply to your particular business?	_____
10. Have you found out what licenses and permits you'll need?	_____
11. Do you know how to make use of trademarks, patents, and copyrights to protect your business?	_____
12. Have you estimated the costs involved in structuring your business and complying with government regulations?	_____
13. Have you consulted with an attorney and obtained the necessary legal advice to set up your business properly?	_____

6

Recordkeeping

Maintaining good financial records is a necessary part of doing business. The increasing number of government regulations alone makes it virtually impossible to avoid keeping detailed records. But just as important as the need to keep records for the government is the need to keep them for yourself. The success of your business depends on them.

THE VALUE OF GOOD RECORDS

An efficient system of recordkeeping can help you to:

- Make management decisions.
- Compete in the marketplace.
- Monitor performance.
- Keep track of expenses.
- Eliminate unprofitable merchandise.
- Protect your assets.
- Prepare your financial statements.

By substituting facts for guesswork and continuity for confusion, day-to-day accounting records enable you to keep your finger on the pulse of your business. Any sign of financial ill health can be detected quickly and the appropriate corrective action taken before it's too late.

Business owners sometimes feel that recordkeeping is an unjustifiable waste of time when a good memory is all that's really needed. Unfortunately, memories can fail. Besides, the business owner can't always be around when an employee needs to check an important piece of information. Taking time to set up and maintain your accounting system can actually save time by bringing order out of chaos. Instead of having to hunt for the financial information you need, or develop it on the spot, you already have it in hand, waiting to be used:

- Last month's sales total.
- Sales commissions paid out in the past two weeks.
- Overtime charges for the previous quarter.
- Advertising expenses for the month.
- Percentage of sales made on credit.
- Customers behind on their bills.
- Amount of money tied up in inventory.
- Inventory shortages.
- Slow moving merchandise.
- Effects of inflation on profits.
- Financial obligations coming due.
- Total value of your assets.

This information, and more, can readily be obtained from an adequate records system. The question isn't whether your business can afford to have one. Rather, it's whether your business can afford *not* to have one.

Accountants. Once the importance of recordkeeping has been recognized, new business owners are often quick to delegate total responsibility for their records to accountants. Pleading ignorance ("What do *I* know about accounting?") or lack of time ("I can either run the business or keep the books."), they dissociate themselves entirely from the accounting function. And why not? After all, that's what accountants are paid for, isn't it? The problem with this tactic is that it gives your accountant free rein to make decisions affecting your business without receiving any input from you. Aside from the fact that this is an open invitation to your accountant to embezzle funds from the business, or use its assets for personal gain, there is an even greater reason for you to keep close tabs on your records system: You can't operate efficiently without access to its information.

For the best results, you and your accountant should work together as a team, supplying each other with accurate and timely information. Whether your accountant handles all your recordkeeping or just does your taxes, it's vital that you understand what is being done.

SETTING UP THE BOOKS

The first steps in setting up the books for your business is to determine which information to keep and which to discard. A good accounting system gives you only the information you need, not a lot of extraneous details.

Accounts. The foundation on which your recordkeeping system is built is your accounts. Each account represents a single category of business transactions (sales volume, rent expense, employees' wages, cash, notes payable). Any changes (increases or decreases) that occur within a specific category are shown in the appropriate account. In this way, when a sale is made, a bill is paid, or an expense incurred, you have a record of it.

In its simplest form, an account looks like the T account below. All cash flowing into your business is entered on the left side of the cash account. All cash flowing out of your business is entered on the right side. Rather than changing the balance each time cash is added or subtracted, the account mechanism enables you to derive your new balance by simply totaling the two sides and subtracting right

T ACCOUNT

CASH		
Increases		Decreases
Beginning Balance $15,000		$600
3,000		250
500		6,350
1,200		
700		
$20,400		$7,200
New Balance $13,200		

CASH ACCOUNT

ACCOUNT *Cash*   ACCOUNT NO. *101*

DATE		ITEM	DEBIT	DATE		ITEM	CREDIT
19XX Aug	1	Balance	15 000 00	19XX Aug	1	Accounts Payable	6 00 00
	2	Sales	3 000 00		2	Supplies	2 50 00

from left to get the difference. This not only saves time, but allows you to see the separate entries that affected the balance.

In comparison to what a regular account looks like, the T account is just the bare outline or skeleton, lacking details. Your actual accounts will probably look something like the accompanying cash account. The basic structure of the T account is still intact, but the refined format enables you to record more information.

Charts of accounts. As you go through the process of determining which accounting information to keep, the names of each account to be included in your records system should be added to your chart of accounts. This identifies your accounts by title and indicates their locations within the system. For example, the cash account in the illustration on page 68 is numbered 101. This means that it falls under the assets category (arbitrarily assigned the number 10) and is the first account within that section. Depending on the number of accounts you wish to maintain, your numbering system can range from the simple to the sophisticated.

Double-entry accounting. For every transaction that is recorded, *two* entries are required. This is because any change in one account automatically results in a change in another account. For instance, if a customer purchases merchandise from you and pays cash for it, the balance in your cash account increases and at the same time your merchandise inventory decreases. Both changes must be recorded. The means for doing this is by way of debit and credit entries. In double-entry accounting, for each transaction *the total debit amount must equal the total credit amount.* If for any reason these amounts aren't equal, the transaction has been recorded incorrectly.

How debits and credits work. There are two common misconceptions about debits and credits. One is to think of them as being good things or bad things (as in "the firefighter was credited with rescuing the child from the burning building" or "that's one more

SAMPLE CHART OF ACCOUNTS

(10) *Assets (Debit)*	(30) *Capital Accounts (Credit)*
101—Cash	301—Owners' capital
102—Accounts receivable	302—Undistributed capital
103—Inventory	
104—Materials and supplies	(40) *Revenues (Credit)*
105—Prepaid expenses	401—Retail sales
106—Land	402—Wholesale sales
107—Buildings	403—Sales—service
108—Reserve for depreciation	404—Miscellaneous income
Buildings (Cr)	
109—Furniture and fixtures	(50) *Expenses (Debit)*
110—Reserve for depreciation	501—Accounting
Furniture and fixtures (Cr)	502—Advertising
111—Automotive equipment	503—Depreciation
112—Reserve for depreciation	504—Insurance
Automotive equipment (Cr)	505—Interest
	506—Miscellaneous
(20) *Liabilities (Credit)*	507—Payroll
201—Accounts payable	508—Rent
202—Notes payable	509—Repairs
203—Sales taxes—payable	510—Supplies
204—FICA taxes—payable	511—Travel
210—Long-term debt—SBA loan	512—Utilities

debit against you"). The other misconception is that "debit" means to "subtract" and "credit" means "to add." Although the outcome of the debit or credit entry can be good or bad and call for addition or subtraction, the terms themselves have much simpler meanings.

- *To debit* is to make an entry on the *left side* of the account.

- *To credit* is to make an entry on the *right side*.

DEBIT AND CREDIT ENTRIES

Type of Account	To Increase the Account Enter the Amount as a	To Decrease the Account Enter the Amount as a
Asset	Debit*	Credit
Liability	Credit*	Debit
Capital	Credit*	Debit
Revenue	Credit*	Debit
Expense	Debit*	Credit

    *Typical account balance

Depending on which account is receiving the entry, both debits and credits can be either positive (calling for an increase) or negative (calling for a decrease). The accompanying chart illustrates this.

Single-entry accounting. Although a double-entry accounting system offers the greatest degree of accuracy through its use of checks and balances, it can also be a difficult system to maintain for someone without bookkeeping experience. Thus, while your business is just starting out or is still small, you may prefer to use a single-entry accounting system instead. Based on your income statement, rather than your balance sheet, a single-entry system does not require you to "balance the books" or record more than one entry for each transaction. Quick and easy to use, it provides a simple way to keep track of your accounts receivable, accounts payable, depreciable assets and inventory.

Depending on your needs, you can have an accountant or bookkeeper set up a single-entry accounting system specially tailored to your business or you can purchase a ready-made system from an office supply or stationery store. Generally consisting of worksheets bound together in a spiral notebook, these ready-to-use systems usually cost less than $15. The most popular system is the one put out by Dome Publishing Company.

Pegboard recordkeeping. To simplify your recordkeeping even more, you might consider using a pegboard recordkeeping system. It's a single-entry system, but its design and the way you use it put it in a category by itself. An all-in-one system for keeping records, writing checks, and issuing receipts, it derives its name from the fact that the checks and receipts it uses are overlaid, one after another, on top of your record sheets and held in place by pegs. Whenever you write a check or a receipt, the information is automatically transferred to the record sheet below. This eliminates the most common accounting error of all—forgetting to record an entry. For more information on pegboard systems, which range in price from $75 to $200, check the *Yellow Pages* under "Business Forms and Systems."

Whether you opt for a single-entry or a double-entry accounting system, the important thing is to have some means for adequately tracking the financial information necessary for your business.

THE ACCOUNTING PROCESS

Entering information into your accounts is neither the first part of the accounting process nor the last. As shown in the chart, the process begins with the business transaction itself and continues

THE ACCOUNTING PROCESS

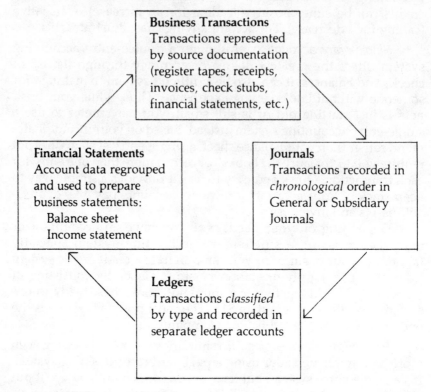

until your financial statements have been prepared. Then the cycle begins again.

Journals

Once a transaction has occurred, information about it enters your accounting system through your journals. Often called the books of original entry, journals are merely *chronological* records of your business transactions. Each entry contains (1) the date on which the transaction occurred, (2) the specific accounts to be debited and credited, and (3) the amount of the debit and credit.

Although one *general journal* covering all transactions is sometimes sufficient for a small business, the majority of businesses also maintain two additional journals: one for cash receipts and one for cash payments. Keeping separate journals serves three main purposes: (1) it saves time, (2) it saves space, and (3) it reduces errors. These savings stem from the fact that, unlike the general journal, the separate journals offer the following benefits:

1. *Headings are preprinted.* Thus less time is spent in recording the necessary information.
2. *Entries require fewer lines.* Thus an entry that takes up three lines in the general journal will require only one line in the cash receipts journal.
3. *Column* totals, *rather than separate entries, are transferred later.* Reducing the number of entries to transfer also reduces the number of possible errors.

Source Documents for Journal Entries

Each entry that is recorded in your journals must be backed up by the appropriate *source document*—in other words, the written evidence, or business paper, that supports the entry. Examples of source documents are sales receipts, invoices, purchase orders, checks, check stubs, register tapes, credit memos, petty cash slips, and business statements. These are necessary not only for tax reporting purposes, but because they provide an additional safeguard against accounting errors and employee dishonesty.

Ledgers

To further consolidate the information contained within your journals and make it more meaningful, the next step in the accounting process is to transfer it to your ledgers. These are the books, files, or computer records in which individual accounts are maintained.

All accounts can be grouped together in one general ledger, or, in addition to this, you may want to set up subsidiary ledgers such as an accounts receivable or an accounts payable ledger to house specific categories of high-activity accounts. The advantage is that these subsidiary ledgers make the general ledger less bulky and allow more than one person at a time to work on the ledger accounts. In place of each group of accounts removed from the general ledger a *control sheet*, summarizing the group's activity, is inserted. This enables the general ledger to stay in balance by maintaining the equality of the debits and credits.

The process of transferring the information in the journals to the ledger accounts is called *posting*. During this stage all data of the same kind are separated from the other journal data and entered into their respective accounts. Since the information recorded in each ledger stems from the journals, ledgers are called books of secondary entry.

To facilitate the process of entering information into your jour-

GENERAL JOURNAL

DATE		ACCOUNT TITLE		DEBIT	CREDIT
1980 NOV	1	Cash		50000	
		Office Equipment			5000
		Receipt No. 1201			
	1	Accounts Payable		32500	
		Cash			32500
		Check No. 1151			
	1	Cash		70000	
		Owners Capital			70000
		Receipt No. 1202			
	1	Cash		65000	
		Sales			65000
		Receipt No. 1203			
	1	Cash		12500	
		Accounts Receivable			12500
		Receipt No. 1204			
	2	Rent Expense		72500	
		Cash			72500
		Check No. 1152			
	2	Advertising Expense		25000	
		Cash			25000
		Check No. 1153			

nals and posting it to the appropriate ledger accounts, there are a number of accounting software programs designed with small businesses in mind. These computer *spreadsheet* programs can assist you not only in keeping your day-to-day records, but also in preparing your financial statements.

Financial Statements

Even though your journals alone are sufficient to give you a complete record of your business transactions, without the ledger accounts to categorize that information, it's virtually unusable. To further increase the value of your accounting data, financial statements are also necessary. These make up the topic of the next chapter.

CASH RECEIPTS JOURNAL

DATE		ACCOUNT TITLE	DOC. NO.	GENERAL DEBIT	GENERAL CREDIT	SALES CREDIT	ACCOUNTS RECEIVABLE CREDIT	CASH DEBIT
1980 NOV	1	Office Equipment	R1201		5000			5000
	1	Owners Capital	R1202		70000			70000
	1	Sales	R1203			65000		65000
	1	Accounts Receivable	R1204				12500	12500

CASH PAYMENTS JOURNAL

DATE		ACCOUNT TITLE	Check No.	GENERAL DEBIT	GENERAL CREDIT	ACCOUNTS PAYABLE DEBIT	CASH CREDIT
1980 NOV	1	Accounts Payable	1151			325.00	325.00
	2	Rent Expense	1152	725.00			725.00
	2	Advertising Expense	1153	250.00			250.00

ACCOUNTS RECEIVABLE CONTROL SHEET

DATE		ITEM	DEBIT	CREDIT	DEBIT BALANCE
1980 Oct	29	Balance			9950.00
	29		150.00		10100.00
	30		300.00	225.00	10175.00
	31			140.00	10035.00
Nov	1			125.00	9910.00

ACCOUNTS RECEIVABLE LEDGER

NAME   Steve Long   TERMS   2/10, n/30
ADDRESS   648 Fifth Street   Torrance, Calif.

DATE		ITEM	DEBIT	CREDIT	DEBIT BALANCE
1980 Oct	1	Balance			85.00
	6	Sales Check #345	65.00		150.00
	15	Sales Check #384	50.00		200.00
	21	Sales Check #395	35.00		235.00
	31	Balance			235.00
Nov	1	Received on Account		125.00	110.00

RECORDKEEPING CHECKLIST

To help ensure that your business transactions are properly recorded and measure the effectiveness of your records system, answer the questions in the Recordkeeping Checklist. Any *no* answers indicate areas that need to be examined.

	Answer Yes or No
1. Do you know the reasons for keeping good records?	_____
2. Have you determined which records are important to your business?	_____
3. Are you using a chart of accounts to show the name and location of each account in your records system?	_____
4. Do you understand the reasoning behind the use of double-entry recordkeeping?	_____
5. Is the function of debits and credits clear to you?	_____
6. Can you identify the accounts likely to have debit balances?	_____
7. Can you identify the accounts likely to have credit balances?	_____
8. Have you set up your general journal and any subsidiary journals that will be used?	_____
9. Do you know what source documents are?	_____
10. Is each journal entry made solely on the basis of a source document?	_____
11. Does your filing system enable you to retain and locate all relevant source documents?	_____
12. Have you set up your general ledger and any subsidiary ledgers that will be used?	_____
13. Is information posted to your ledgers periodically?	_____
14. Are all ledger items based on journal entries?	_____
15. Are financial statements prepared at periodic intervals?	_____
16. Do you personally oversee all major business transactions?	_____
17. Are you thoroughly familiar with all aspects of your accounting systems?	_____

**Answer
Yes or No**

18. Does your accounting system enable you to operate your business efficiently and get the full value out of your resources?   _____

19. Are you able to verify the following through your records?
    Cash on hand at the end of the day   _____
    All money owed to you by customers
    Accounts that are past due   _____
    All money owed to suppliers and creditors
    Bills that have been paid   _____
    Inventory that has been received
    Salary and wages paid
    All other expenses that have been incurred

20. Have you obtained the advice of an accountant in setting up your records system?   _____

7

Financial Statements

The information obtained through your system of financial recordkeeping is only as good as your ability to use it. In addition to compiling your financial data, you must also know how to summarize and interpret it.

SUMMARIZING FINANCIAL DATA

Summarizing involves taking the information contained within your ledger accounts and using it to prepare the financial statements for your business. The two most important of these are the balance sheet and the income statement (often referred to as a profit and loss statement, or P&L).

The *balance sheet* is a summary of your business's assets, liabilities, and capital on a given day.

The *income statement* is a summary of your business's income and expenses during a specific period (month, quarter, year).

The difference between these statements can be compared to the difference between a photograph and a motion picture. The balance sheet is like a photograph, depicting your business as it appears in a single instant. The income statement is like a motion picture, depicting your business as it changes over time. Since financial statements are prepared annually (or more often, as desired), it's common to see balance sheets dated "December 31, 19XX" and income statements dated "For the year ended December 31, 19XX."

THE IMPORTANCE OF FINANCIAL STATEMENTS

Unlike day-to-day accounting records, financial statements provide an overview of your business. Instead of telling what you sold on a particular day, or how much a specific inventory item cost, financial statements give you the big picture—comparing what you own to what you owe, what you earned to what you spent. As such, they form the basis for any financial analysis of your business.

Financial statements are absolutely essential for the following:

- **Management planning.** To operate your business in the most profitable way possible, or lay the groundwork for future expansion, you need to know where your business stands and how it got there.
- **Raising capital.** Bankers and investors use financial statements as a way of evaluating your business. If you wish to obtain the support of either group, you must not only supply statements, but be ready to explain and defend them.
- **Preparing tax returns.** The information contained within your financial statements is needed to prepare your tax returns. Furthermore, in the event of an audit by the Internal Revenue Service, you will be expected to produce the relevant accounting records and statements.

THE BALANCE SHEET

A balance sheet has two main sections, one listing the assets of the business and one listing the liabilities and capital of the business. In accordance with the accounting equation, the two sides are always equal:

$$\text{Assets} = \text{Liabilities} + \text{Capital}$$

This can be readily explained by the fact that all assets in a business are subject to the claims of creditors and owners.

Assets

An asset is anything of monetary value that is owned by the business. Assets are generally classified as being (1) current, (2) fixed, or (3) intangible. The order in which they appear on the balance sheet

THE STATIONERY STORE DECEMBER 31, 19XX		
Assets		
Current Assets		
Cash		$15,000
Accounts receivable	$36,000	
Less allowance for bad debts	(1,500)	
		34,500
Inventory (at cost)		46,500
Total current assets			$ 96,000
Fixed Assets		
Furniture and fixtures	33,000	
Delivery van	30,000	
		63,000
Less accumulated depreciation		(3,000)
Total fixed assets			60,000
Total assets			$156,000
Liabilities and Capital		
Current Liabilities		
Accounts Payable	$27,000	
Notes payable (due within 1 year)	12,000	
Accrued liabilities	3,000	
Total current liabilities		$42,000
Long-Term liabilities		
Notes payable (due after 1 year)		12,000
Total current liabilities			$ 54,000
Capital		
Owner's capital, January 1, 19XX		99,000
Net income for year	45,000	
Less proprietor's drawings	(42,000)	
Undistributed income		3,000
Total capital, December 31, 19XX			102,000
Total Liabilities and Capital			$156,000

is determined by their *liquidity*—that is, their ability to be converted into cash.

Current assets. These consist of cash and assets that are expected to be converted into cash within the coming year. Included in this category are accounts receivable (money owed by customers) and inventory (merchandise, supplies, raw materials, and parts).

Fixed assets. These consist of tangible property to be used over a period of years in operating the business. Included in this category are land, buildings, machinery, equipment, motor vehicles, furniture, and fixtures.

Intangible assets. These consist of items that are usually non-physical assets. Included in this category are trademarks, patents, copyrights, and goodwill.

Liabilities

A liability is a debt owed by the business. Liabilities are classified as being either current or long-term.

Current liabilities. These consist of debts that are expected to be paid off within the coming year. Included in this category are accounts payable (money owed to suppliers and creditors), notes payable (money owed to the bank), and accrued liabilities (wages, interest, taxes, deposits, and other amounts due but not paid as of the balance sheet date).

Long-term liabilities. These consist of those debts that are *not* due to be paid within the coming year. Included in this category are mortgages, term loans, bonds, and similar future obligations.

Capital

The difference between the assets of a business and its liabilities equals its capital:

$$\text{Assets} - \text{Liabilities} = \text{Capital}$$

Capital represents the amount of owner investment in the business, as well as any profits (or losses) that have accumulated.

Sole proprietorship or partnership. In a sole proprietorship or partnership, capital is listed under each owner's name. Increases (or decreases) in capital are also shown there.

Corporation. In a corporation, capital is listed under the heading "Capital stock." This represents the paid-in value of the shares of stock issued to each owner. Corporate earnings that are not distributed to shareholders are shown here as "Retained earnings."

THE INCOME STATEMENT

An income statement (or profit and loss statement) can generally be divided into the following sections:

- Net sales.
- Cost of goods sold.
- Gross margin.
- Expenses.
- Net income (or loss).

Together, these demonstrate both the extent and the efficiency of the business's ability to generate income during the accounting period covered by the statement.

Net sales represents the total sales during the accounting period, *less* sales tax and deductions for sales discounts, returns, or allowances.

Cost of goods sold represents the total amount spent by the business to purchase the products sold during the accounting period. Businesses usually compute this by adding the value of the goods purchased during the period (less discounts offered by suppliers) to the value of the beginning inventory, and then subtracting the ending inventory.

Gross margin represents the difference between the net sales and the cost of goods sold. It is also frequently referred to as the *gross profit*.

Expenses represent costs incurred as a result of operating the business. These can be divided into two categories—*selling expenses* (expenses, such as sales commissions and advertising, that are directly related to the business's sales activities) and *general and administrative expenses* (expenses incurred through activities other than selling, such as clerical salaries, rent, and insurance).

SAMPLE INCOME STATEMENT

THE STATIONERY STORE FOR THE YEAR ENDING DECEMBER 31, 19XX			
			Percent
Net Sales		$300,000	100%
Cost of Goods Sold			
Inventory, January 1		$ 46,500	
Purchases	$153,300		
Less cash discount	(2,400)		
		150,900	
Available for sale		197,400	
Less inventory,			
December 31		(47,400)	
Cost of goods sold		150,000	50
Gross Margin		150,000	50
Expenses			
Accounting and legal		3,000	
Advertising		7,500	
Depreciation		3,000	
Insurance		3,500	
Interest		2,500	
Miscellaneous		7,500	
Payroll		36,000	
Rent		25,500	
Repairs		1,500	
Supplies		4,500	
Travel		6,000	
Utilities		4,500	
Total expenses		105,000	35
Net Income		$ 45,000	15

Net income represents what's left after all relevant expenses have been deducted from the gross margin. When total expenses exceed the gross margin, this is called a *net loss*.

INTERPRETING FINANCIAL DATA

Interpreting financial data involves studying the various relationships that exist among the figures shown on your financial statements. These relationships are expressed in the form of *financial ratios*, comparative measurements that enable you to pinpoint the strengths and weaknesses in your business operations.

What if you needed to know the answer to one or more of the following questions?

- Is there enough ready cash in my business?
- Are current liabilities at a safe level?
- How well could the business weather a financial setback?
- Are customers paying their bills on time?
- Is inventory moving as quickly as it should be?
- Are prices keeping pace with inflation?
- Are profits what they should be?
- Are assets being used wisely?
- How much of my business do I really own?

How could you get your hands on the necessary information? Call your accountant? Sure, if you had the time and the money to spend waiting for an answer. But why bother when the information is already right at hand, in your financial statements? Solving a few quick arithmetic problems is all it takes to find the answers.

Financial ratios can be used to find out a great deal of information about your business, ranging from the trivial to the significant. Among the ratios most closely examined by the owners, investors, and creditors are those pertaining to (1) liquidity, (2) profitability, and (3) ownership.

Liquidity Ratios

These measure your business's ability to pay its bills and to convert assets into cash.

Current ratio. This ratio, which compares current assets to current liabilities, is used to assess your business's ability to meet its financial obligations within the coming year. The best known and most widely used of the ratios, it's computed by dividing current assets by current liabilities:

$$\text{Current ratio} = \frac{\text{Current assets}}{\text{Current liabilities}}$$

$$\text{Current ratio} = \frac{\$96{,}000}{\$42{,}000}$$

$$\text{Current ratio} = 2.29{:}1$$

The generally acceptable minimum current ratio is 2 to 1. This can vary, though, depending on the specific circumstances of each business.

Acid-test ratio.   This ratio, which compares cash and accounts receivable to current liabilities, is used to assess your business's ability to meet its current financial obligations in the event that sales decline and merchandise inventory cannot readily be converted to cash. Also called the *quick ratio* because it measures only ready assets, it's computed by dividing cash and accounts receivable by current liabilities:

$$\text{Acid-test ratio} = \frac{\text{Cash} + \text{Accounts receivable}}{\text{Current liabilities}}$$

$$\text{Acid-test ratio} = \frac{\$15,000 + \$34,500}{\$42,000}$$

Acid-test ratio = 1.2:1

An acid-test ratio of 1 to 1 is considered acceptable, given the fact that an adequate means of collecting accounts receivable exists.

Working capital ratio.   This ratio, which compares current assets and current liabilities, is used to assess your business's ability to meet unforeseen expenses or weather a financial setback. It's computed by subtracting current liabilities from current assets:

Working capital = Current assets – Current liabilities
Working capital = $96,000 – $42,000
Working capital = $54,000

Working capital needs vary from business to business. Frequently, though, lenders will insist that the level of working capital be maintained at or above a minimum level.

Average collection period, which compares your average day's sales to accounts receivable, is used to assess your business's ability to convert accounts receivable into cash. It's computed in a two-step process that *first* divides net sales by the number of days in the year; in the *second* step, this figure (the average day's sales) is divided into accounts receivable:

Step 1

$$\text{Average day's sales} = \frac{\text{Net sales}}{365 \text{ Days}}$$

$$\text{Average day's sales} = \frac{\$300,000}{365}$$

Average day's sales = $822 per day

Step 2

$$\text{Average collection period} = \frac{\text{Accounts receivable}}{\text{Average day's sales}}$$

$$\text{Average collection period} = \frac{\$34,500}{\$822 \text{ per day}}$$

Average collection period = 42 days

What average collection period is acceptable depends on the credit terms. Generally, it should not exceed $1\frac{1}{3}$ times the credit terms. Thus, since the Stationery Store offers 30 days credit, its average collection period is slightly higher than it should be ($1\frac{1}{3} \times 30 = 40$ days).

Inventory turnover compares your cost of goods sold to your average inventory level. Average inventory level is calculated as half the total of beginning inventory plus ending inventory. Inventory turnover is used to assess your business's ability to convert merchandise inventory into sales. It's computed by dividing the cost of goods sold by the average inventory:

$$\text{Inventory turnover} = \frac{\text{Cost of goods sold}}{\text{Average inventory}}$$

$$\text{Inventory turnover} = \frac{\$150,000}{\frac{1}{2}(\$46,500 + \$47,400)}$$

$$\text{Inventory turnover} = \frac{\$150,000}{46,950}$$

Inventory turnover = 3.2 times

Normally, the higher your turnover is, the better. This means you're moving the goods. However, as the turnover rate increases, so does the risk of stock shortages. By trial and error and by studying the turnover rates of similar businesses, you can determine what rate is desirable for your business.

Profitability Ratios

These measure your business's ability to use its assets to make a profit.

Net profit on sales compares net profit to net sales. Used to assess your business's ability to turn a profit on the sales it makes, it's computed by dividing net profit by net sales:

$$\text{Net profit on sales} = \frac{\text{Net profit}}{\text{Net sales}}$$

$$\text{Net profit on sales} = \frac{\$45,000}{\$300,000}$$

Net profit on sales = 0.15 or 15%

In this example, the Stationery Store makes 15 cents profit for every dollar in sales. Whether this is an acceptable level of profit depends on your objectives and the standard for your industry.

Return on investment (ROI) compares net profit to total assets. Used to assess your business's ability to turn a profit on the assets it holds, it's computed by dividing net profit by total assets:

$$\text{Return on investment} = \frac{\text{Net profit}}{\text{Total assets}}$$

$$\text{Return on investment} = \frac{\$45,000}{\$156,000}$$

Return on investment = 0.29 or 29%

To determine if this is a good return on investment, you should compare your figures to those of comparable businesses.

Ownership Ratio

This measures the levels of ownership in the business, comparing owners' claims to those of creditors.

Worth to debt compares net worth to total debt. It's used to assess your business's ability to protect creditors against losses. To compute it, divide net worth by total debt:

$$\text{Worth to debt} = \frac{\text{Net worth}}{\text{Total debt}}$$

$$\text{Worth to debt} = \frac{\$102,000}{\$54,000}$$

$$\text{Worth to debt} = 1.89:1$$

For every dollar lent to the Stationery Store the owner has invested $1.89. Usually a ratio of 2 to 1 or better is preferred since this provides creditors with more protection. To improve this ratio, the owner can either invest more money in the business or reduce his debt.

As you can see, calculating the financial ratios for your business can be done fairly easily. To make it even easier and to more readily compare one set of ratios with another, there are several financial software programs on the market that you can use.

FINANCIAL RATIO CHECKLIST

Once you have prepared the financial statements for your business, you can pinpoint its financial strengths and weaknesses by computing the ratios in the following Financial Ratio Checklist.

	Ratio	Satis-factory	Unsatis-factory
Liquidity			
Current ratio	_____	_____	_____
Acid-test ratio	_____	_____	_____
Working capital	_____	_____	_____
Average collection period	_____	_____	_____
Inventory turnover	_____	_____	_____
Profitability			
Net profit on sales	_____	_____	_____
Return on investment	_____	_____	_____
Ownership			
Worth to debt	_____	_____	_____

8

Obtaining Capital

Prior to commencing operations, you will want to estimate as realistically as possible the amount of capital needed to launch and sustain your business during its first three to six months. This is your initial investment. Since it takes a while before revenues exceed or even equal expenses, a financial cushion is essential in your estimate. The cushion can mean the difference between success and failure, enabling you to meet payroll and supplier obligations, make loan payments, and keep your doors open until the business is fully self-supporting.

A common mistake of first-time entrepreneurs is in neglecting to take into account such invisible costs of operating a business as insurance, deposits or bonds, license fees, estimated sales taxes, and membership dues in professional organizations. If added after the fact, these "incidentals" could easily throw the best of budgets out of kilter.

Your own personal financial needs must also be considered. Not only does your business need capital in order to survive during the first months of operations, but so do you. To be accurate, your estimated initial investment must include an allowance adequate to support yourself while you are establishing your business. This allowance can be in the form of either a salary or drawing account privileges.

DETERMINING YOUR INITIAL INVESTMENT

For a Retail Operation

The first step in detemining the amount of your initial investment is to estimate your projected annual sales volume. This is based on such factors as the type and size of your intended business and its location. Any previous related business experience that you may have, combined with the most up-to-date research you can find, will be invaluable here. The more you know about your new business, the more you will know what to expect.

Once you have computed your sales volume for the year, it's easy to work backward to figure out the dollar investment necessary to meet your starting merchandise inventory requirements. This is done by dividing estimated sales volume by inventory turnover (the number of times per year that your merchandise will sell out). For instance, if your estimated annual sales volume is $300,000 and you expect to turn over your merchandise three times per year, then your initial merchandise inventory should last four months and have a retail value of $100,000. At cost, given a 50-percent markup, this would amount to an initial investment of $50,000.

Although merchandise inventory turnover varies by industry and by merchandising techniques (high-volume retailer versus specialty store), the average turnover for your type of business can be ascertained by referring to Robert Morris Associates *Statement Studies* or Dun & Bradstreet's *Key Business Ratios*, both available at most libraries. For additional information, make it a point to consult with prospective suppliers too.

INITIAL INVESTMENT FOR A RETAIL OPERATION

Starting inventory at cost		$ 50,000
Furniture and fixtures		
Purchase price (if paid in full)		12,000
Cash down payment (if purchased on contract)		4,500
Fees for legal, accounting, licenses, and other		
preopening expenses		3,750
Expenses (for 4 months, 1 turnover period)		
Payroll	$ 9,000	
Rent	8,400	
Other	16,600	
Total expenses		34,000
Contingencies		3,750
Total initial investment		$108,000

Now that you have estimated your initial merchandise inventory costs, the next step is to estimate the amount of money required to meet all other costs during your first turnover period. These include rent, insurance, furniture and fixtures, supplies, salaries, utilities, and advertising. Remember to cushion your projections. When added to your merchandise inventory costs, these will give you the total initial investment required for your business.

For a Nonretail Operation

If you are starting a manufacturing company or service establishment, the method of calculating your initial investment will need certain minor revisions. The major difference between a manufacturer and a retailer is that the bulk of the manufacturer's initial investment doesn't go for merchandise; it goes for machinery, which will be used for several years, and for raw materials, which can be converted into finished goods. Furthermore, a manufacturer must make such key decisions as whether to lease equipment and whether to manufacture or purchase the component parts of the product. These decisions will affect the amount not only of your initial investment, but of your taxes as well.

A service establishment, in most cases, requires neither an extensive merchandise inventory nor a large investment in capital equipment. Skills are the main product. As a result, the service establishment is easier to start than either a retailing or manufacturing business and usually calls for a considerably smaller initial investment. This explains in part why the number of businesses categorized as services is increasing at such a rapid rate. Statistics provided by the Labor Department show that service industries will continue to expand and grow for the next ten years.

SOURCES OF CAPITAL

You can turn to a variety of sources to obtain financing for your business. Which ones you choose will depend primarily on the way in which the money is to be used in the business and the degree of ownership you wish to retain.

Capital usage. If a large sum of money is required—such as for the purchase of physical facilities, machinery, or inventory—it's likely that you will want to delay repaying this as long as possible.

Conversely, smaller sums of money to cover operating expenses would normally be repaid within the year.

Debt versus ownership. Whether you borrow the money you need or solicit it from investors will determine your level of ownership in the business. Once you accept a loan, you have an obligation to repay it with interest. But no ownership is transferred to the lender. Investment capital is just the opposite of this. You neither return the investor's money nor pay interest on it. However, the investor becomes a co-owner with you in the business.

In determining the proper balance of debt capital (borrowed money) to equity capital (invested money) that's right for you, you should be aware of two drawbacks. In the case of debt capital, if for any reason you are unable to repay your loans on time, you could easily be forced into bankruptcy. Equity capital, on the other hand, though seemingly risk-free, presents another problem: control. Unlike lenders, investors have a say in how the business should be run. The greater the amount of equity capital you obtain, the greater the amount of ownership you relinquish.

Personal Investment

Your first and most likely source of capital is, of course, yourself. The amount of money you decide to invest in starting a business will depend partly on how much money you have readily available, be it in savings, in investments, or paid into your home. It will also depend on how the ownership in the business is to be divided.

Your chances of avoiding investing any of your own money in the business are slim. Since forming a business involves risk, prospective creditors and investors will expect you, the owner, to share in that risk. However, there are exceptions. If you have a unique idea or valuable skills to contribute to the business, these might augment capital or be an acceptable substitute for it.

Should you be planning to finance your business solely from your own personal resources, on the other hand, you may want to reconsider. Instead of putting the money directly into the business, it would be to your advantage to use it as collateral for a loan to the business. Not only would this build up your credit standing, but, since the interest paid on the loan is tax-deductible expense, the loan would be virtually cost-free.

Family and Friends

Obtaining money from family and friends, through loans or investments, may also be an alternative. But bear in mind that this can strain both your personal and your business relationships unless the proper safeguards are taken.

The provisions for the repayment of such loans should be clearly stated in writing, including the duration of each loan, the interest rate, and the payment schedule. In this way you can minimize future misunderstandings over the nature of the money entrusted to you.

When relatives or friends become investors in your business the terms of this association should be stipulated in advance. How much of a say will they have in running the business? Do you have the right to buy back their interest in the company? How will the proceeds be distributed? All this should be put in writing. If these questions and others are answered in the beginning, problems may be avoided later.

Partners

Others, besides friends and family, may be interested in entering into the business with you. These could be business acquaintances, classmates, or simply entrepreneurs looking for a business opportunity. Forming a partnership with one or more of these interested parties could be the way to fulfill not only your capital requirements but your personnel needs as well. Remember, though, that in so doing you dilute your ownership and lessen the magnitude of your control.

Shareholders

Selling shares of stock in a business as a means of raising capital is an option permitted only to corporations. Should you decide to do so, you must first incorporate. Since this involves obtaining a corporate charter from the state in which your business will be based, it is advisable to consult an attorney for assitance in this matter.

Offsetting the red tape inherent in forming a corporation is the corporation's unique ability to accumulate large sums of capital. Aided by such features as limited liability and easy transfer of stock ownership, the corporation is able to draw on the resources of a vast and diverse pool of investors. Brought together by a common goal— to make a profit—these investors, as shareholders, will have the right to influence corporate policy decisions. However, you can retain control by holding onto a majority of the shares of stock.

Bondholders

In addition to selling stock, corporations are permitted to sell bonds. Unlike shares of stock, which represent ownership in the business, bonds represent debt. In exchange for investing in bonds, bondholders are paid a predetermined interest rate over the life of the bond. This interest differs from dividends in that it is categorized as a business expense and therefore is deductible. When the bond matures (usually in 10 to 30 years) the bondholder receives the principal investment back.

Since bonds are a form of long-term debt, they are more often used to finance major business expansion costs such as the purchase of plant and equipment. Before making the decision to sell bonds, though, it's important that you determine your corporation's future ability to pay the annual interest and retire the bonds when they reach maturity. Furthermore, during the early stages of your business, investors may be understandably reluctant to purchase the corporation's bonds, preferring that you establish yourself first.

Commercial Banks

Despite what you may have heard about how difficult it is to get a bank loan, banks are a major source of capital for new businesses. Prior to approaching your banker for a loan, though, you should be aware of the criteria on which your request will be evaluated. In banking terminology, there are *six Cs of credit:* capital, collateral, capability, character, coverage, and circumstances.

Your banker will want to know how much *capital* your business has to start with and what percentage of it is your own personal investment. What assets do you possess that can be used as *collateral* for the loan? Based on your experience and repuation, a determination will be made regarding your *capability* and *character*. The type and amount of insurance *coverage* you plan to obtain is another important factor. The general *circumstances* of your business (competition, level of consumer demand, current economic environment) will also be taken into consideration.

Your ability to sell your banker on your strengths in each of these areas will directly affect the outcome of your loan application.

So be prepared to provide such back-up information as financial statements, references, market research data, and a detailed plan for achieving your company's objectives. Establishing your creditworthiness in this way makes it much easier to get a yes answer.

Credit Unions

Credit unions generally offer lower interest rates than banks. But to qualify for a loan, you must be a member. If you don't belong to a credit union, you might want to explore the possibility of joining one. Established for the purpose of providing members with low-interest loans, credit unions are usually formed around an employer, professional organization, church, or fraternal group.

The most common types of loans credit unions make are short-term consumer loans for automobiles, furniture, boats, and so on. However, you might be able to stretch these bounds to encompass furnishings for your business, equipment, or a company car. Most credit unions will lend up to $5,000 to purchase a computer. And, if your credit rating is good, you could qualify for a personal signature loan up to $10,000.

Savings and Loan Associations

Savings and loans have traditionally focused their attention on making long-term loans to home buyers and have played only a small role in business financing. Over the years, though, more and more savings and loans have shown an increased interest in making business loans. The reason for this shift is simple. Business loans are normally repaid over a shorter time than home loans; this enables the S&Ls to recoup their money faster. Taking this into consideration, you might want to investigate your local savings and loans to find out which ones are probusiness.

If you own your own home, there's also the possibility that a savings and loan association will give you a loan based on your equity in the home. This route should be pursued with caution, though. Mortgaging your home to obtain business capital can be risky since a business loss could put your home in jeopardy.

Small Business Administration

The Small Business Administration (SBA) is a federal agency, created in 1953 to provide business with both advice and financial aid. In this regard, it can make either direct or indirect loans to businesses. A *direct loan* is one made by the SBA itself. An *indirect loan* is a loan made by another lending institution, but guaranteed up to 90 percent by the SBA. Both kinds have lower interest rates and longer maturities than those associated with conventional loans. But the SBA is not in competition with the financial community.

Calling itself the "lender of last resort," the SBA usually works in partnership with lending institutions, making or guaranteeing loans only when other financing isn't available.

In granting loans, the SBA is influenced favorably by the following conditions:

1. The business to be financed is the primary source of income for the family.
2. Financial assistance is not otherwise available on reasonable terms from private sources.
3. A reasonable amount is at stake in the venture. Generally, SBA will want at least 20 percent at stake in a start-up operation.
4. There is reasonable assurance of repayment.
5. The new venture is feasible and sound.
6. The applicant has ability and experience in the area of the business.
7. The applicant is of good character.
8. The borrower agrees not to discriminate in the business on grounds of race, creed, color, or national origin.

Before you attempt to put together a loan application package by yourself, the SBA suggests that you prepare and collect the following information (see the forms and questionnaire at the end of this chapter):

1. Business plan.
2. Personal financial statement.
3. Statement of personal history.
4. Start-up costs.
5. Forecast of profit or loss.

Once you have gathered this information, you should contact your local SBA field office to discuss your business plans further. At that point you will receive advice regarding your proposal and the preparation of a loan package.

Small Business Investment Companies

Small Business Investment Companies (SBICs) are privately owned and operated companies that have been licensed and in some cases financed by the Small Business Administration to provide small businesses with long-term debt and equity financing. The intent of the 1958 Small Business Investment Act, authorizing the formation of SBICs, was to increase the number of private companies willing to invest in small businesses.

Though all SBICs must conform to SBA regulations and are subject to SBA control, they are not all the same. SBICs range from those specializing in the entertainment industry to those in the aerospace field. The preferred method of investment (debt versus equity) and the amount of that investment can also vary. If you are considering SBIC financing, you will therefore want to compare SBICs. To get additional information on SBICs and a list of those near you, contact your local SBA field office.

Supplier Credit

Depending on your credit rating, some suppliers may be persuaded to provide such items as inventory, furniture, fixtures, and equipment on a delayed payment basis. In the case of inventories, full payment would normally be due within 30 days. Furniture, fixtures, and equipment could be paid off over a longer period, perhaps as much as several years.

Supplier credit has two advantages. It allows you to stretch your available cash, and the related interest charges can be deducted from your taxes as business expense. However, since many suppliers offer discounts for early payment, the corresponding disadvantage is that you will be paying higher prices.

Finance Companies

Finance companies make loans that banks and other lenders regard as too risky. Known for their liberal credit policies and speedy loan processing, finance companies make both secured and unsecured loans for virtually any purpose. As such, they provide another business funding alternative—but an expensive one. Proof that convenience comes at a price is the significantly higher interest rates they charge. So, before relying on this source of capital, you should carefully consider your options and what it will cost.

Venture Capital Firms

One of the least known, but nonetheless important, sources of funds for businesses is venture capital firms. These are privately owned investment companies that provide capital to new and growing businesses in exchange for an ownership stake in them. Keenly focused on just one factor—the business's profit potential—venture capitalists generally look for a 25 percent annual return on investment over a five-year period. Their ultimate goal is for the business to "go public," thus enabling them to recoup three to five times their investment by selling shares of stock in the business in a public stock offering.

Venture capital firms are primarily interested in businesses that require an investment between $250,000 and $3 million. However, if an especially promising project requires more than that, a venture capital firm will sometimes increase its investment or join forces with other firms to provide the necessary funds.

If your business has strong growth and profit potential, then venture capital is certainly a financing option to consider. Bear in mind, though, you must be willing to give up part of your equity in the business and to permit investors to have a say in management decisions. By giving up a little, though, you could end up with a lot. It was venture capital that helped two young entrepreneurs—Stephen Wosniac and Steven Jobs—turn their business dream into Apple Computer.

You can find out more about venture capital firms by checking such sources as bankers, accountants, venture capital directories, and business/finance magazines (*Inc., Money, Fortune, Forbes*). Then get your business plan in order. The best way to get a venture capitalist's attention is with a winning business plan.

SBA BUSINESS PLAN QUESTIONNAIRE

The SBA will ask you the following questions as part of their financing procedure:

---

1. Business experience and education?
2. Kind of business? Construction, manufacturing, service, etc. What is your product? Describe the product or service you plan to make or sell.
3. Why did you choose this kind of business?
4. Sole proprietorship, partnership, or corporation?

5. Amount of loan required and anticipated use of funds?

6. Where will the business be located? Why was this location selected?

7. How much capital do you have and what will be invested in the business (briefly)?

8. Have you attended an SBA Pre-Business Workshop?

9. Do you have an accountant or bookkeeping service in mind to set up financial records?

10. What kinds of licensing will you require?

11. How many employees will you need?

12. What kind of insurance will you carry?

SBA START-UP COSTS FORM

Whether you are starting a new business, moving to a new location, opening a new branch, or expanding your business, you will have some "start-up" or one-time expenses. In all applications for such purposes, the following information will be required:

1. Furniture, fixtures, machinery, equipment:
   a. Purchase price (if paid in full with cash) $_____

   b. Cash down payment
      (if purchased on contract) $_____

   c. Transportation and installation costs $_____

2. Starting inventory and supplies $_____

3. Decorating/remodeling/leasehold improvements $_____

4. Deposits
   a. Utilities $_____

   b. Rents/leases $_____

   c. Other (identify) $_____

5. Fees
   a. Legal, accounting, other $_____

   b. Licenses, permits, etc. $_____

   c. Other (identify) $_____

6. Other (working capital, etc.) $_____

                                                          Total $_____

   Less equity injection $_____

   Amount of loan request $_____

PERSONAL FINANCIAL STATEMENT (FRONT)

OMB Approval No. 3245-0188

PERSONAL FINANCIAL STATEMENT

U. S. SMALL BUSINESS ADMINISTRATION

As of_____, 19_____

Complete this form for: (1) each proprietor, or (2) each limited partner who owns 20% or more interest and each general partner, or (3) each stockholder owning 20% or more of voting stock and each corporate officer and director, or (4) any other person or entity providing a guaranty on the loan.

Name

Business Phone (   )

Residence Address

Residence Phone (   )

City, State, & Zip Code

Business Name of Applicant/Borrower

ASSETS (Omit Cents)		LIABILITIES (Omit Cents)	
Cash on hands & in Banks	$	Accounts Payable	$
Savings Accounts	$	Notes Payable to Banks and Others	$
IRA or Other Retirement Account	$	(Describe in Section 2)	
Accounts & Notes Receivable	$	Installment Account (Auto)	$
Life Insurance–Cash Surrender Value Only	$	Mo. Payments $	
(Complete Section 8)		Installment Account (other)	$
Stocks and Bonds	$	Mo. Payments $	
(Describe in Section 3)		Loan on Life Insurance	$
Real Estate	$	Mortgages on Real Estate	$
(Describe in Section 4)		(Describe in Section 4)	
Automobile–Present Value	$	Unpaid Taxes	$
Other Personal Property	$	(Describe in Section 6)	
(Describe in Section 5)		Other Liabilities	$
Other Assets	$	(Describe in Section 7)	
(Describe in Section 5)		Total Liabilities	$
		Net Worth	$
Total . . $		Total . . $	

Section 1. Source of Income		Contingent Liabilities	
Salary	$	As Endorser or Co–Maker.	$
Net Investment Income	$	Legal Claims & Judgments	$
Real Estate Income	$	Provision for Federal Income Tax	$
Other Income (Describe below)*	$	Other Special Debt	$

Description of Other Income in Section 1.

*Alimony or child support payments need not be disclosed in "Other Income" unless it is desired to have such payments counted toward total income.

Section 2.   Notes Payable to Bank and Others.   (Use attachments if necessary. Each attachment must be identified as a part of this statement and signed.).

Name and Address of Noteholder(s)	Original Balance	Current Balance	Payment Amount	Frequency (monthly,etc.)	How Secured or Endorsed Type of Collateral

SBA Form 413 (5–91) Previous Editions Obsolete. Ref: SOP 50–10 and 50–30   (tumble)

PERSONAL FINANCIAL STATEMENT (BACK)

Section 3. **Stocks and Bonds.** (Use attachments if necessary. Each attachment must be identified as a part of this statement and signed).

Number of Shares	Name of Securities	Cost	Market Value Quotation/Exchange	Date of Quotation/Exchange	Total Value

Section 4. **Real Estate Owned.** (List each parcel separately. Use attachments if necessary. Each attachment must be identified as a part of this statement and signed).

	Property A	Property B	Property C
Type of Property			
Name & Address of Title Holder			
Date Purchased			
Original Cost			
Present Market Value			
Name & Address of Mortgage Holder			
Mortgage Account Number			
Mortgage Balance			
Amount of Payment per Month/Year			
Status of Mortgage			

Section 5. **Other Personal Property and Other Assets.** (Describe, and if any is pledged as security, state name and address of lien holder, amount of lien, terms of payment, and if delinquent, describe delinquency).

Section 6. **Unpaid Taxes.** (Describe in detail, as to type, to whom payable, when due, amount, and to what property, if any, a tax lien attaches).

Section 7. **Other Liabilities.** (Describe in detail).

Section 8. **Life Insurance Held.** (Give face amount and cash surrender value of policies – name of insurance company and beneficiaries).

I authorize SBA/Lender to make inquiries as necessary to verify the accuracy of the statements made and to determine my creditworthiness. I certify the above and the statements contained in the attachments are true and accurate as of the stated date(s). These statements are made for the purpose of either obtaining a loan or guaranteeing a loan. I understand FALSE statements may result in forfeiture of benefits and possible prosecution by the U.S. Attorney General (Reference 18 U.S.C. 1001).

Signature:	Date:	Social Security Number:
Signature:	Date:	Social Security Number:

PLEASE NOTE: The estimated average burden hours for the completion of this form is 1.5 hours per response. If you have questions or comments concerning this estimate or any other aspect of this information, please contact Chief, Administrative Branch, U.S. Small Business Administration, Washington, D.C. 20416, and Clearance Office, Paper Reduction Project (3245–0188), Office of Management and Budget, Washington, D.C. 20503.

*U.S. Government Printing Office: 1991 — 282-429/45503

STATEMENT OF PERSONAL HISTORY

OMB APPROVAL NO. 3245-0178
Expiration Date. 5-31-90

Please Read Carefully - Print or Type

Each member of the small business concern requesting assistance or the development company must submit this form in TRIPLICATE for filing with the SBA application. This form must be filled out and submitted by:

United States of America

SMALL BUSINESS ADMINISTRATION

STATEMENT OF PERSONAL HISTORY

1. If a sole proprietorship by the proprietor.
2. If a partnership by each partner.
3. If a corporation or a development company, by each officer, director, and additionally by each holder of 20% or more of the voting stock.
4. Any other person including a hired manager, who has authority to speak for and commit the borrower in the management of the business.

Name and Address of Applicant (Firm Name) (Street, City, State and ZIP Code)	SBA District Office and City
	Amount Applied for.

1. Personal Statement of (State name in full, if no middle name, state (NMN), or if initial only, indicate initial). List all former names used, and dates each name was used. Use separate sheet if necessary	2. Date of Birth: (Month, day and year)
First Middle Last	3. Place of Birth: (City & State or Foreign Country)
	U.S. Citizen? ☐ YES ☐ NO If no, give alien registration number:

| 4. Give the percentage of ownership or stock owned or to be owned in the small business concern or the Development Company. | Social Security No. |

5. Present residence address:	City	State
From: To: Address:		
Home Telephone No. (Include A C):	Business Telephone No. (Include A/C)	
Immediate past residence addres:		
From: To: Address:		

BE SURE TO ANSWER THE NEXT 3 QUESTIONS CORRECTLY BECAUSE THEY ARE IMPORTANT.

THE FACT THAT YOU HAVE AN ARREST OR CONVICTION RECORD WILL NOT NECESSARILY DISQUALIFY YOU. BUT AN INCORRECT ANSWER WILL PROBABLY CAUSE YOUR APPLICATION TO BE TURNED DOWN.

6. Are you presently under indictment, on parole or probation?

☐ Yes ☐ No   If yes, furnish details in a separate exhibit. List name(s) under which held, if applicable

7. Have you ever been charged with or arrested for any criminal offense other than a minor motor vehicle violation?

☐ Yes ☐ No   If Yes, furnish details in a separate exhibit. List name(s) under which charged, if applicable.

8. Have you ever been convicted of any criminal offense other than a minor vehicle violation?

☐ Yes ☐ No   If Yes, furnish details in a separate exhibit. List name(s) under which convicted, if applicable.

9. Name and address of participating bank

The information on this form will be used in connection with an investigation of your character. Any information you wish to submit, that you feel will expedite this investigation should be set forth.

Whoever makes any statement knowing it to be false, for the purpose of obtaining for himself or for any applicant, any loan, or loan extension by renewal, deferment or otherwise, or for the purpose of obtaining, or influencing SBA toward, anything of value under the Small Business Act, as amended, shall be punished under Section 16(a) of that Act, by a fine of not more than $5000, or by imprisonment for not more than 2 years, or both.

Signature	Title	Date

It is against SBA's policy to provide assistance to persons not of good character and therefore consideration is given to the qualities and personality traits of a person, favorable and unfavorable, relating thereto, including behavior, integrity, candor and disposition toward criminal actions. It is also against SBA's policy to provide assistance not in the best interests of the United States, for example, if there is reason to believe that the effect of such assistance will be to encourage or support, directly or indirectly, activities inimical to the Security of the United States Anyone concerned with the collection of this information, as to its voluntariness, disclosure or routine uses may contact the FOIA Office. 1441 'L' Street, N.W. and a copy of §9 'Agency Collection of Information' from SOP 40 04 will be provided

SBA FORM 912 (5-87) SOP 9020 USE 6-85 EDITION UNTIL EXHAUSTED

Please Note: The estimated burden hours for completion of this form is 15 minutes per response. If you have any questions or comments concerning this estimate or any other aspect of this information collection please contact, Chief Administrative Information Branch, U.S. Small Business Administration 409 Third Street, S.W. Washington, D.C. 20416 or Gary Waxman, Clearance Officer, Paperwork Reduction Project (3245-0178), Office of Management and Budget, Washington, D.C. 20503

1. SBA FILE COPY

PROJECTED PROFIT/LOSS

	%	J	F	M	A	M	J	J	A	S	O	N	D	Total
Total net sales														
Cost. goods sold														
Gross														
Controllable expense														
Salaries/wages														
Payroll taxes														
Legal/Accounting														
Advertising														
Automobile														
Office supplies														
Dues/Subscriptions														
Telephone														
Utilities														
Miscellaneous														
Total Con. Exp.														
Fixed Expenses														
Rent														
Depreciation														
Insurance														
Licenses/Permits														
Taxes														
Loan Payments														
Total Fixed Exp.														
Total Expenses														
Net profit/Loss (before tax)														

FINANCING CHECKLIST

To get a better idea of the amount of capital you need and to find out if you have thoroughly researched the avenues of financing that are open to you, answer the questioins in the following Financing Checklist.

	Answer Yes or No
1. Have you determined the amount of initial investment required for your business?	_____
2. Did you include a financial cushion in your estimate?	_____
3. Have you decided how much of your own money to put into the b usiness?	_____
4. Have you weighed the pros and cons and debt versus ownership financing?	_____
5. Have you investigated each of these sources of capital?	
Family	_____
Partners	_____
Shareholder	_____
Bondholders	_____
Banks	_____
Savings and loan associations	_____
Credit unions	_____
Small Business Administration	_____
SBICs	_____
Suppliers	_____
6. Have you spoken to your banker about obtaining a loan?	_____
7. Would you give yourself a positive rating in each of the six Cs of credit?	
Capital	_____
Collateral	_____
Capability	_____
Character	_____
Coverage	_____
Circumstances	_____
8. Are you aware of the SBA's criteria for granting loans?	_____
9. Have you explored the possibility of obtaining SBIC financing?	_____
10. Have you spoken to an accountant regarding the various financing options open to you?	_____

9

Controlling Your Inventory

Every business, regardless of whether its primary function is retailing, wholesaling, services, or manufacturing, has one thing in common: inventory. In fact, the major portion of your investment dollars is likely to go for inventory. Included in this are expenditures for merchandise, supplies, raw materials, and parts, all of which are expected to earn profits for your business. To do so, however, they must be kept in proper balance. This is the aim of inventory control.

A good inventory control system does four things:

1. It keeps inventory at the optimum level.
2. It orders goods in the most economical quantities.
3. It speeds up merchandise turnover.
4. It reduces inventory shrinkage.

In other words, it enables you to get maximum value out of your inventory at minimum cost. But if it can do all that, it must be complicated, right? Not really. Actually, it's pretty simple. Just as a thermostat is keyed to react to changes in temperature, an inventory control system reacts to changes (or the lack of changes) in your level of inventory. Once you've set up the system, it's almost totally automatic.

THE OPTIMUM LEVEL OF INVENTORY

Many businesses mistakenly abide by the philosophy that the more inventory you have on hand, the better, as a way of making sure that no sales are lost. What they don't realize is that the costs of carrying the extra inventory could more than equal the "profits" from the additional sales. Added to the cost of the inventory itself are the costs of shipping, storage, insurance, and taxes. And there's always the danger that the inventory will become obsolete before it can be used or sold. That's a high price to pay for the security of having your shelves full.

Adopting a let-them-eat-cake attitude isn't the solution either. Purposely letting your business run short on the inventory used for operations activities or sales is guaranteed to alienate customers and employees alike. Among the costs incurred as a result of inventory shortages are:

• Special handling charges and sacrificed purchase discounts, because of the need to place rush orders.

• Underutilization of personnel, equipment, and facilities.

• Lost sales.

When sales are involved, your loss can be far-reaching. This is because dissatisfied customers have a tendency to take their future business elsewhere.

This brings us to your objective—the optimum level of inventory. What is it? It's the level of inventory that is the most profitable. Rather than eliminating the costs of stock shortages altogether, or reducing inventory carrying costs to the lowest possible figure, it results in the lowest *total* of the two.

For example:

Inventory Level	Costs of Stock Shortages	Costs of Extra Inventory	Total
A	$1,000	$8,750	$9,750
B	$2,500	$6,500	$9,000
C	$3,750	$4,000	$7,750
D	$5,500	$3,000	$8,500

The optimum level at which to maintain inventory is level C, since this reduces the total cost by the greatest amount.

Once you've established, through trial and error, the optimum level of inventory for your business, it's up to your control system to keep it at that level. This is accomplished by (1) measuring the goods on hand, (2) indicating the amounts needed, and (3) calculating delivery times.

Measuring the Goods on Hand

This is the way to find out what you have and what you don't have. Does that carton on the top shelf contain a dozen widgets, as marked, or is it empty? There are three ways to find out: Make an educated guess, open the carton and count what's inside, or check your records.

1. Educated guess. This method relies on your memory and powers of observation to determine what's in stock. In the event that your business is small and you're able to keep close tabs on the day-to-day operations, it might be fairly accurate. But there's also a good chance it could be wrong. To be on the safe side, you should do a physical count at least once a year.

2. Physical count. The most accurate, albeit time-consuming, way to monitor your inventory levels is to do a physical count. This means tallying the goods on hand at periodic intervals to make sure that your estimated inventory matches up with your actual inventory.

3. Perpetual inventory. A perpetual inventory system records changes in stock as they occur. Using the information obtained from stock tags, receipts, and requisition forms, the appropriate stock number, size, color, and so on are entered into the inventory filing system at the time the goods are received, used, or sold. This can be done manually or by computer. When using this system, supplement it with a physical count one or more times per year. (See the perpetual inventory file card.)

Indicating the Amounts Needed

Having determined the extent of your inventory, you've reached the crucial point in the control process—deciding what to order and how much. This is where the automatic feature of your inventory control system comes into action. Based on your estimates of the minimum

PERPETUAL INVENTORY FILE CARD

Description _____ Location _____
Supplier _____ Reorder point _____
EOQ _____

Received		Sold		Balance	
Date	Amount	Date	Amount	Date	Amount

of the minimum quantities of goods that are required to keep your inventory in balance, the system is programmed to react to specific *reorder points*. Each reorder point represents the level at which an inventory item needs to be replenished. The actual amount to be purchased is determined by such information updates as:

- Changes in operations activities.
- Changes in customer preferences.
- Changes in seasons.
- Changes in products (improved, discontinued, and so on).
- Changes in profit margins.
- Changes in suppliers.

For instance, if the customer demand for a particular item is starting to taper off, you might decide to let that item drop below its reorder point without purchasing additional stock.

Calculating Delivery Times

The success of your inventory control system hinges on your ability to calculate delivery times. How long will it take the supplier to fill your order—not just to verify it over the phone, but actually process the paperwork, pack the goods, and deliver them to your place of business? Unless the goods are on your shelves when you need them, not merely somewhere in transit, your hope of maintaining a balanced inventory is slight.

The way to minimize foul-ups in deliveries is to maintain good supplier relations. This means familiarizing yourself with each supplier's delivery capabilities (lead time needed, special order policy, dependability, and so on) so that you know what to expect. It also means keeping your requests within reason (not "I need it yesterday"). When suppliers find that you have an understanding of their business operations, they are more inclined to take an interest in yours. If this policy fails and you get poor service, don't be afraid to switch suppliers.

ECONOMIC ORDER QUANTITY

In addition to keeping your inventory at the optimum level, it's the function of your control system to determine the *economic order quantity* for each item. This is the number of units you must order so as to achieve the lowest total cost. Using your reorder points and estimated demand levels as a springboard, you already know what to order and how much. And you know the delivery capabilities of your suppliers. But should you place one large order? Several small orders? A few medium-sized orders? What's the most economical order quantity?

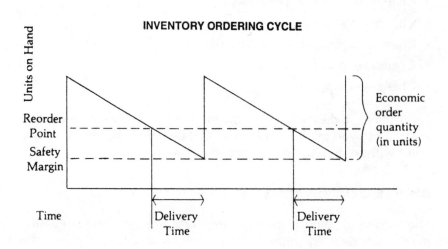

INVENTORY ORDERING CYCLE

The economic order quantity can be arrived at by offsetting the costs associated with each order. For instance, the larger your order, the greater your inventory carrying costs, but the smaller your ordering and delivery costs. Conversely, with small orders your carrying costs decrease and delivery costs go up.

At first, coming up with a winning combination might seem a little like trying to balance on a teeter-totter—by yourself. Fortunately, you can use a formula to calculate the right answer:

$$\text{Economic order quantity} = \overline{\dfrac{2SC}{IP}}$$

where S = sales (in units) for the period

C = cost of ordering (clerical, shipping, etc.)

I = inventory carrying charge (storage, insurance, taxes), expressed as a percent of inventory value

P = price per unit

Thus if S = 5,000 units

C = $50

I = 15%

P = $25

$$EOQ = \overline{\dfrac{2SC}{IP}}$$

$$EOQ = \overline{\dfrac{2 \quad 5,000 \quad \$50}{0.15 \quad \$25}}$$

$$EOQ = \overline{\dfrac{\$500,000}{\$3.75}}$$

$$EOQ = \overline{133,333}$$

$$EOQ = 365 \text{ units}$$

The hardest part of ascertaining the EOQ is figuring out the square root at the end. But don't let that discourage you from using the formula. An electronic calculator or square root table can solve the problem. Or you can use a computer inventory control program to do the calculations. Whichever method you choose, once you have determined the economic order quantity for a specific item, it isn't necessary to recalculate it each time you oder unless there are changes in demand, costs, or delivery capabilities.

Purchase Discounts

In calculating the economic order quantities of the inventory items you need, it's important to pay close attention to purchase discounts. These are price reductions made available by suppliers on the basis of order size, total purchases per period, order season, or credit terms.

1. Order size. A discount is given when a larger order is placed. This encourages customers to order in larger quantities, thus reducing the supplier's shipping and handling costs, while increasing revenues.

2. Total purchases. A discount is given as the total amount of your purchases per period increases. This is done to stimulate repeat buying.

3. Order season. A discount is given when your order is placed prior to the peak ordering season. In this way suppliers can even out demand levels and reduce storage requirements.

4. Credit terms. A discount is given when prompt payment is made for goods that have been received. The most commonly offered discount is 2/10, net 30. This authorizes you to deduct 2 percent from your bill if payment is made within ten days; otherwise you are expected to pay the full amount in 30 days.

By taking advantage of these discounts, you can further reduce your ordering costs. However, this doesn't mean that you should purchase more than you need or can afford in an effort to save money. Each inventory item purchased should be justified on its own merits, exclusive of any accompanying discounts.

MERCHANDISE TURNOVER

Your inventory control system can help you speed up merchandise turnover in a variety of ways. These include:

- Improving purchasing methods.
- Monitoring inventory levels.

- Identifying hard-to-move items.
- Adjusting for seasonal demand.
- Recognizing trends.

Rather than waiting till you're stuck with an oversupply of any one item, an effective system alerts you to the potential inventory problem before it happens. This enables you to stay on top of things by cutting back orders if necessary, modifying display and sales techniques, reducing markups, or increasing promotional efforts.

UNIVERSAL PRODUCT CODES

If your inventory control system is equipped to make use of bar code data, so much the better. *Bar codes*, or *universal product codes* (UPCs), as they are officially called, are the vertical lines on packages and price tags that get scanned at electronic cash registers when a purchase is made. Along with telling you the price of an item sold, a bar code can help you to control your inventory by providing such information as the item's:

- Stock number.
- Size.
- Color.
- Category/department.
- Season.

When this data is scanned at the register and entered into your inventory control system, you can get a good idea of what's moving and what's not.

Although retailers are the greatest users of bar code data, manufacturers and others are making use of it too, using it to process customers' orders, track inventory as it moves through the production process, and monitor workers' output. The only drawback to using UPC codes is the price of the electronic equipment. But, just as with computers, this has been steadily dropping. So more and more small businesses are now utilizing UPC codes as an inventory control/accounting tool. For more information on UPC codes, contact:

Universal Product Code Council
8163 Old Yankee Rd., Suite J
Dayton, OH 45458
(800) 543-8137

JUST-IN-TIME MANAGEMENT

Borrowing an idea from the Japanese, an increasing number of manufacturers and service providers, such as furniture manufacturers and film processing labs, are using an inventory control technique called *just-in-time* (JIT) management. Rather than optimizing inventory levels, this method seeks to virtually eliminate them. This involves calculating inventory delivery times right down to the day, or even to the hour, when the supplies are needed. Then the shipment is ordered to be delivered at that precise time. Upon arrival, the inventory goes directly to the work station where it's needed and is immediately utilized. This method can be difficult to put into practice. But, when it's successful, it reduces inventory storage and handling costs and gives businesses greater flexibility in adapting to customers' needs, resulting in increased productivity—and profits.

To make just-in-time work in your business, you'll have to know your inventory needs to the letter and hone your supplier relations to a fine edge. Cooperation is the key. It also helps to be located in close proximity to suppliers to facilitate deliveries.

INVENTORY SHRINKAGE

Inventory shrinkage refers to unaccountable stock shortages. Inventory that should be in your stockroom or on your shelves may just disappear. This can be caused by employee or customer theft, misplaced stock, or simply poor recordkeeping. Whatever the reason, missing inventory can be a source of frustration and mystification to the business owner, who often feels powerless to stop it.

One way to combat shrinkage is to tighten security. But the effectiveness of this method will be diluted unless it is backed up by inventory control. To reduce shrinkage, the following inventory controls are recommended:

- Inventory shipments should be logged in when received.
- Purchase orders and invoices should be properly filed.
- Requisition forms should be used to keep track of the supplies, materials, and parts used in operating your business.
- A record should be kept of all sales transactions.
- A physical inventory should be taken at least once each year.
- Perpetual inventory figures should be matched against physical inventory results.

These will help you to prevent most inventory shrinkage from occurring and to detect it quickly when it does occur.

INVENTORY CHECKLIST

To find out whether your inventory control system is doing all the things it's supposed to do, answer the questions in the following Inventory Checklist.

	Answer Yes or No
1. Do you have an adequate system for monitoring your level of inventory?	_____
2. Is a physical count taken at least once a year?	_____
3. Have you determined the optimum level of inventory for your business?	_____
4. Have you established reorder points for replenishing inventory items?	_____
5. Do you make adjustments for changes in customer demand when placing orders?	_____
6. Are you familiar with suppliers' delivery capabilities?	_____
7. Do you order in the most economic quantities?	_____
8. Do you take advantage of purchase discounts?	_____
9. Do you keep track of slow moving stock?	_____
10. Can you spot potential fast movers?	_____
11. Is your merchandise inventory balanced by price line, color, size, and type?	_____
12. Do you select merchandise items with your target customers in mind?	_____
13. Are you taking preventive action against inventory shrinkage?	_____
14. Is your inventory as profitable as it should be?	_____

10

Setting the Price

In setting the prices for your products and services, among the facts to be considered are the reactions of your customers, the stiffness of the competition, and the state of the economy. Strange as it may seem, a price that's too low can be just as much of a turn-off to customers as a price that's too high. Low prices are often interpreted as signifying low value or inferior merchandise. As for the competition, since your business doesn't exist in a vacuum, the role of other businesses in influencing your prices has to be recognized. Whether you decide to go head-to-head with competitors on prices, matching them dollar for dollar, or to undercut them, or to charge higher prices is crucial to your pricing. Nor can the state of the economy be overlooked. Unemployment, inflation, interest rates, government policies, and levels of investment all have an effect on consumer spending and therefore on your prices.

You must also take into consideration another factor: profit. If your prices are so low that they fail to cover your expenses, or so high that an insufficient number of people want to buy from you, the result is a loss of profits. Your goal is to meet the demands of customers, keep an eye on competitors and the economy, and assure yourself of satisfactory profits.

PRICING AND CUSTOMERS

Part of knowing what prices to charge comes from knowing your customers. One customer's bargain may be another's extravagance.

Affluent customers generally demand high-quality merchandise, personalized service, and an exclusive and attractive environment in which to shop. In exchange for these amenities, they are not only willing to pay more, but *expect* to pay more. Low-income customers, on the other hand, are primarily concerned with stretching their dollars. They're willing to settle for less quality and service and a no-frills, discount house type of environment in exchange for lower prices. In each case the price is what counts.

In the beginning, formulating a price strategy to please your customers may seem like trying to solve the riddle of the chicken and the egg. Which comes first? Should you set your prices and then wait for your target customers to find you? Or should you wait to see what kind of customers you attract, and then develop an appropriate pricing strategy? The answer is both. To a great extent your pricing strategy will be predetermined by your type of business, location, target customers, expenses, and so on. But you also have to stay in touch with your customers to make sure that your prices, quality, and service continue to reflect their needs and wants.

PRICING AND COMPETITION

Keeping tabs on competitors' prices helps you to assess your own pricing strategy. Are yours higher or lower than the competition? If your prices are higher, you're probably losing out on sales. If your prices are lower, you may be making more sales but passing up additional profits. In comparing your prices with the competition, don't forget to compare service as well. Services add to the value of a product and therefore to its price. Such services as a prestige location, attractive facilities, personal attention, credit, gift wrapping, validated parking, warranties, and home deliveries benefit your customers. The more services you provide, the higher your prices are likely to be.

Here are some of the sources of information you can use to stay in touch with competitors' pricing strategies.

Customers. Observing customers' shopping habits and listening to what they have to say can give you a pretty good idea of how your prices stack up against the competition.

Suppliers. Since *your* suppliers are also *their* suppliers, this is another source of competitive information. But don't forget that the information flows both ways. Your competitors can tap into the same source to find out about you.

Advertising. Following competitors' promotional campaigns enables you to keep track of pricing changes and also obtain current information about the quality and service being provided.

Competitors' catalogs and price lists. When these are available, they are an excellent source of information, particularly since the prices are not only current but conveniently arranged for easy reference.

Price checkers. These are shoppers employed by you to go out and gather information about competitors' prices. While pretending to shop, they actually record the prices of various key items.

PRICING AND THE ECONOMY

Customer shopping habits reflect the state of the economy. During a recession or depression, customers are at their most price-conscious. Worried about the high cost of living, threats of unemployment, and cutbacks in credit, they want to make every dollar count. As the economy improves, customers become more optimistic about the future and are more willing to pay higher prices. When the economy is at its peak and business is booming, customers offer little resistance to rising prices. The general feeling is that there's more money where that came from, so why not spend it?

As a business owner, your ability to recognize these fluctuations in the economy and to adjust your prices accordingly adds to your competitiveness. To keep your prices in line with customers' expectations, you may add or drop services, raise or lower quality standards, change your markups, or put together some combination of these.

PRICING AND PROFIT

Your prices should be set at a level sufficient to reimburse you for the cost of the goods or services sold, cover your overhead costs, and provide a profit. The amount of profit you receive will be dependent on your gross margin, or *markup*. This is the difference between the cost and the selling price of the goods sold. The higher the markup, the greater your profit *per sale*. However, this doesn't necessarily mean that your overall profits will be higher. Why? Because higher markups usually result in reduced sales. This explains why discount stores are able to make healthy profits despite lower-than-average markups; their sales volume is higher.

PRICING METHODS

There are a number of pricing methods to choose from, ranging from the simple to the complex. Here are three of the most used methods.

1. *Competitive pricing.* Prices are set at or below the competition's. Costs are made to conform to the prices that have been set.
2. *Standard markup pricing.* A standard markup is computed and then added to the cost of the goods or services sold. Some businesses apply a single markup across the board, while others have different markups for each sales category.
3. *Cost-oriented pricing.* Prices are set individually, based on the cost of the goods or services sold, the overhead, and the desired profit.

Of the three methods, cost-oriented pricing is the most accurate but also the most complex and time-consuming, since each product or service is evaluated separately. A standard markup saves time by eliminating the need to do individual computations. For a store that carries hundreds or thousands of merchandise items, this can make a big difference. Competitive pricing is the simplest method of all. Prices are virtually preset, being based on what's acceptable for your industry.

Common sense and a little experimentation will soon tell you which method or combination of methods works best for you. If you're in a highly competitive industry where the key determinant of sales is the price, you'll have little choice but to use the competitive pricing method. For businesses with extensive inventories, time considerations alone will dictate that some sort of standardized markup be used. The cost-oriented pricing method is normally used by business offering one-of-a-kind products or specialized services.

MORE ABOUT MARKUPS

If you aren't careful in computing markups, you can easily shortchange yourself. A common mistake among new business owners is to forget to include all relevant expenses in the final figure. As a result, potential profits are eaten up and sometimes even converted into losses. Your markup needs to cover all administrative expenses, all selling expenses, and all losses stemming from merchandise discounts, theft, or damage. In addition, it has to provide a measure of profit.

This holds true regardless of which pricing method you use. In the standard markup method, these cost and profit considerations are all built into the markup figure itself. With cost-oriented pricing, they are added as you go. And in competitive pricing you work backward from the price to figure the markup.

Markup to Price

You can determine what your selling price would be, given a particular markup, by using this formula:

$$\text{Selling price} = \frac{\text{Cost of goods or services}}{100 - \text{Markup}} \quad 100$$

For instance, if a man's suit costs $160 and your markup is 50 percent, you would calculate the selling price as follows:

$$\text{Selling price} = \frac{\$160}{100 - 50} \quad 100$$

$$\text{Selling price} = \$320$$

Price to Markup

If you're considering a particular price and want to know what the amount of your markup would be, you can figure that out too:

$$\text{Markup} = \frac{\text{Selling price} - \text{Cost}}{\text{Selling price}}$$

Using the cost and selling price from the previous example, the markup would be calculated like this:

$$\text{Markup} = \frac{\$320 - \$160}{\$320}$$

$$\text{Markup} = \frac{\$160}{\$320} = 50\%$$

Avoiding percentages altogether, many retailers use a method called the *keystone markup*, which entails simply doubling the cost of an item to obtain its selling price. Although quick and easy, this method obviously can't be used in all situations.

PRICING STRATEGY

Now that you have the basics, it's time to consider strategy. If pricing were just a matter of plugging different numbers into a formula and coming up with the right figure, it wouldn't require any strategy at all—just a good head for numbers. This isn't the case. In addition to mathematical ability, you need marketing savvy.

Market Response: Elasticity

The first thing you need to find out is how responsive your market is to a change in price. This responsiveness is called *elasticity*. Products such as eggs, baking soda, razor blades, and medicine are highly *inelastic*. Regardless of whether their prices are raised or lowered, customers continue to purchase them in approximately the same quantities. Customer demand for some products, on the other hand, fluctuates with the price. A small change in price—up or down—results in a decrease or increase in the number of units sold. This type of response is said to be *elastic*. For example, television sets, strawberries, clothing, and jewelry are highly elastic.

As a rule, items that are considered to be necessities are less elastic than those that are considered to be luxuries. This is because the customer's need, rather than the product's price, triggers the purchase. For instance, a person with a headache doesn't wait until aspirin is on sale before buying it. The need to get rid of the headache takes priority over the price.

How does all this affect your pricing strategy? For one thing, the more inelastic your product is, the easier it is to raise your prices without hurting your sales. That means more profits on the same volume. To increase your profits on highly elastic products, rather than raising your prices you might try lowering them. Although this reduces your profit on each unit sold, the resultant increase in sales volume should increase your overall profits.

Other Determinants of Price

In addition to product elasticity, other pricing determinants include:

- Volume.
- Image.
- Consumer psychology.
- Product life span.
- Profit objectives.

Volume.   Are you selling to a mass market or just an elite few? High-volume businesses generally employ low markups. Conversely, the lower your volume is, the higher the markup you'll need to cover your overhead and provide a profit.

Image.   Do you want your business known for its quality or for having the best buys? If you're after a quality image, you may decide to use a *prestige* pricing strategy. This strategy calls for deliberately setting prices high in order to attract affluent customers. The opposite of prestige pricing is *leader* pricing. Used to draw large numbers of customers into a store, leader pricing emphasizes low-priced specials that have common appeal. Two-for-one sales and cents-off coupons are typical of this.

Customer psychology.   According to market researchers, consumers react more favorably to certain prices than others. An item selling for $9.95 or even $9.99 has a better chance of being purchased than the identical item at $10. Even though the difference in price is insignificant, psychologically it makes a difference.

Product life span.   What's the life span of your product? If you're selling fashion or *fad* items (string bikinis, pet rocks) that appeal to customers for only a brief time, you need to make your profits quickly. Otherwise, you could be left holding a bagful of expenses when the demand drops off. The longer your product's life span, the longer the period of time you have in which to earn your profits. This explains the numerous claims by advertisers that their products are new and improved. For the most part, such assertions are nothing more than attempts to stretch a product's life span and extend profits.

Profit objectives.   In formulating pricing strategy, the key thing to remember is not to lose sight of your overall objective: maintaining profitability. This may mean taking a loss on one product to stimulate the sales of another (leader pricing). It can also call for changes in your method of operation (high volume versus low volume).

Marketing Mix

Just as your business doesn't exist in a vacuum, neither do your pricing decisions. Price is only one of the four components that make up the *marketing mix*. The others—product, place, and promotion—must all be in harmony with the prices you set. The products and services you decide to sell, your distribution system, and the messages you communicate about your business directly influence your pricing strategy and profitability.

Based on your marketing mix objectives, you may want to employ one or more of the following pricing strategies:

- Skimming.
- Penetration.
- Price-lining.
- Promotional pricing.
- Price bundling.
- Time period pricing.
- Value-added pricing.
- Captive pricing.

Skimming. Used for new, innovative products that are just being introduced into the marketplace, a skimming strategy calls for you to set your price high in the beginning and then to lower it over time as a product becomes more widely accepted. The advantage of this approach is that it enables businesses to quickly recoup their research, development, and promotion costs. It is most often used for high-tech consumer electronics and computer products, or for high-fashion or fad products with short life spans.

Penetration. This strategy involves pricing your products low and keeping the prices low in an effort to penetrate the market and gain wide distribution and consumer acceptance. Since it entails shrinking your profit margins, this strategy only works with low-cost products that can be mass produced and are capable of achieving high sales volumes. This strategy is usually employed for low-tech, frequently purchased items, such as soft drinks, soap, and candy bars.

Price-lining. Businesses employing this strategy categorize their products within different price ranges, or *lines* (high, medium, low), and price them accordingly. A clothing retailer, for example, may carry men's ties that sell for under $12, $12.95–$24.95, and over

$25. Depending on what customers are willing to spend, they can then choose from the preferred price range. This method makes it easier for businesses to price and display their products—and for customers to buy them.

Promotional pricing. As the name implies, this strategy offers lower, "limited time only" prices on specific products to stimulate sales. It can be utilized for special purchase items that were bought at a discount or linked to customers' buying times (holidays, seasons, events, and so on). Lowering the price of hot dogs and buns during the World Series or having a special promotion on patio furniture during the summer are examples.

Price bundling. This strategy consists of "bundling" separate products or services together and selling them as a package. For example, a hotel might offer a "fun and sun" package that includes lodging, meals, and bicycle rentals. Other bundled price packages include dinner "combos" (entree, dessert, and beverage), beauty kits containing cosmetics products, and flashlights sold with batteries.

Time period pricing. This strategy raises or lowers prices based on consumer demand levels at various times, charging higher prices at peak times and lower prices during slow times. "Early bird" restaurant specials and off-season travel discounts are examples.

Value-added pricing. A business using this strategy offers an additional service or gift when a customer makes a regularly priced purchase. Widely used in the cosmetics field, other examples of value-added pricing include offering a maintenance contract with a computer system, a T-shirt with a pair of running shoes, or a book with a magazine subscription.

Captive pricing. With this pricing strategy, you set your price low on one product, then make your profit by selling customers other products that go with it. Selling low-price razors to make money on the blades is a classic example. Utilizing this approach, a weight-loss clinic might offer low-price memberships in the clinic to make money selling food supplements and prepared meals to members (a captive market).

These are just some of the most frequently used pricing strategies. By taking a creative approach, you should be able to adapt them to your own needs or to come up with other pricing strategies that are uniquely suited to your business.

PRICING STRATEGY CHECKLIST

For help in developing your pricing strategy and keeping it on target, answer the questions in the following Pricing Strategy Checklist. Afterward, compare your answers to see if there are any inconsistencies in your overall pricing strategy.

	Answer Yes or No
1. Do you try to evaluate the market forces affecting the demand for your products?	_____
2. Have you considered what price strategies would be compatible with your total marketing mix?	_____
3. Do you know which products are slow movers and which are fast?	_____
4. Do you know which products are elastic and which are inelastic?	_____
5. Do you know your competitors' pricing strategies?	_____
6. Are you influenced by competitors' price changes?	_____
7. Do you regularly review competitors' ads to update your information on their prices?	_____
8. Is your store large enough to employ a comparison shopper?	_____
9. Is there a specific time of year when your competitors have sales?	_____
10. Do your customers expect sales at certain times?	_____
11. Would periodic special sales, combining reduced prices and heavier advertising, be consistent with the store image you are seeking?	_____
12. Should any leader offerings (selected products with quite low, less profitable prices) be used?	_____
13. Will cents-off coupons be used in newspaper ads or mailed to selected consumers on any occasion?	_____
14. Will odd-ending prices, such as $9.95 or $9.99, be more appealing to your customers than even-ending pricing?	_____
15. Have you determined whether to price below, at, or above the market?	_____
16. Do you determine specific markups for each product?	_____

17. Do you use standardized markups for product
    categories?

    _____

18. Are your prices set so as to cover the full costs on every
    sale?

    _____

19. Are additional markups called for, because of increases,
    or because an item's low price causes consumers to
    question its quality?

    _____

20. Should employees be given purchase discounts?

    _____

21. Should any group of customers, such as students or
    senior citizens, be given purchase discounts?

    _____

11

Staffing

The most valuable asset of any business is its people. Land, buildings, merchandise, and equipment may dominate a balance sheet, but they don't make a business successful; people do. The best businesses are the ones that have the best people—capable, creative, energetic people. To attract them requires both ingenuity and initiative on your part. But the payoff in productivity is worth it. Staffing your business with the best people available should be one of your highest priorities.

Placing a sign in your window saying, "Help wanted, apply within" is one way to get results—but not necessarily the results you want. A sign in the window will probably bring in a stream of applicants. But unless they possess the skills to do the job, a great deal of time can be wasted in interviewing and you still would not find anyone you want to hire. Generally, the sign in the window works only when the position to be filled calls for little or no skills and entails a minimum amount of responsibility. How then should you go about hiring the people you need? First it's important to realize that hiring is only one element in staffing. This is an ongoing process that involves finding qualified people, hiring them, making the best use of their skills and abilities, and having them stay on the job instead of quitting and taking their talents elsewhere.

The steps you must take *before* you hire anyone are to (1) analyze each job, (2) prepare job descriptions, (3) check recruitment sources, (4) utilize application forms, (5) conduct interviews, and

(6) verify information. *After* the hiring decision is made, you have to (1) provide job orientation, (2) provide training, (3) evaluate performance, (4) compensate employees, and (5) monitor employee turnover. By following these steps, instead of waiting for fate to send you perfect employees or complaining about your current employees, you can control and direct the staffing process.

ANALYZE EACH JOB

This is the most important step in staffing since it forms the basis for any hiring decisions that you make. Unfortunately, it's often skipped over by employers who, in a rush to get a position filled quickly, would rather hire now and ask questions later. Then, when confronted with poor performance, low morale, and high turnover, they wonder why it's so hard to find good workers any more. Taking a little more time in the beginning is the way to avoid a great many problems later.

During the job analysis step you should ask yourself:

- What work has to be accomplished?
- Do I need additional help to do it?
- How many people do I need?
- Would part-time help be sufficient?
- What skills am I looking for?
- How much experience is required?
- Is the labor market favorable?
- How much am I able to pay?

You may find that you don't need to hire anyone after all. Perhaps, if you reschedule the work flow or juggle work assignments, your present staff can handle it. Or you may find out that one additional person isn't enough. Maybe you need to hire two or more people to keep pace with the workload. Or a job you thought anyone can do may in fact require someone with specific skills. The answer to your questions can be surprising. But that's the point of doing a job analysis. It's better to be surprised before you hire someone, rather than after. The choice is yours. You can be the one saying, "If only I'd known," or you can take the time to find out.

PREPARE JOB DESCRIPTIONS

A *job description* is a written record of the duties and responsibilities associated with a particular job. It serves a dual purpose, making it easier for you to match the right person to the right job and informing each employee of what his/her job entails.

In preparing a job description, include the following details:

- A general description of the job.
- The duties to be performed.
- The job responsibilities.
- Specific skills needed.
- Education and experience required.

For instance, a receiving clerk in a store might have a job description that looks like the sample shown below. Once you've put everything down on paper, you're ready to start looking for the person who fits the description.

SAMPLE JOB DESCRIPTION

Job Title: Receiving clerk

Supervisor: Store owner

Summary: Responsible for receiving shipments from suppliers. Removes goods from containers and places them on warehouse shelves. Prepares and processes paperwork and maintains receiving files.

Duties and responsibilities:

- Removing stock from containers and placing merchandise on warehouse shelves.
- Checking invoices to merchandise received.
- Inspecting merchandise received.
- Typing miscellaneous forms and labels.
- Maintaining receiving files.
- Assisting in physical inventory.
- Keeping warehouse clean and orderly.

Job Specifications:

- Education: High school graduate
- Experience: None required
- Skills: Must be able to organize material; work with numbers; interact well with people.

CHECK RECRUITMENT SOURCES

The method of recruitment that you decide to utilize depends on your business. Waiters and waitresses might easily be recruited from your local high school. Finding qualified real estate brokers or skilled carpenters calls for a different method. Some of the sources to choose from are:

- Public employment agencies.
- Private employment agencies.
- Newspaper advertisements.
- Local schools.
- Unions.
- Trade and professional associations.

Public employment agencies. Public employment agencies operate throughout each state, finding and placing both blue-collar and white-collar workers. Without charge, they will recruit and screen job applicants, sending you only the ones who meet your specifications.

Private employment agencies. Private employment agencies operate much the same as public ones do, except that there is a fee involved. Either you pay it or the person who is hired pays it.

Newspaper advertisements. A newspaper advertisement enables you to reach a large pool of interested job applicants quickly. However, it's important to design your ad in such a way as to attract those who are qualified, while discouraging the unqualified. The way to do this is to (1) make it interesting, (2) give adequate details about the job, (3) indicate the skills needed, and (4) specify the education and experience. A general guideline is to stick to a straightforward approach, since cute or exaggerated copy tends to generate a negative reaction.

Local schools. Contacting the placement centers at local high schools and colleges is a good way to find applicants who are long on potential, though usually short on experience. If you're looking for part-time help, this source should particularly be considered.

Unions. For a number of jobs, ranging from plumbers to publicists, the way to recruit qualified personnel is to go through their respective unions. In some instances, this is your only alternative.

Trade and professional associations. Most trade and professional associations are eager to assist employers in obtaining the services of their members. Whether you need help in finding an accountant, sales manager, management trainee, computer specialist, or supervisor, the local association is a good place to check.

As your business grows, other recruitment sources such as employee referrals, previous job applications on file, and industry contacts will become increasingly useful.

UTILIZE APPLICATION FORMS

Job application forms simplify the hiring decision by helping you screen out unsuitable applicants and focus on qualified ones. The application can also serve as a starting point during an interview, suggesting questions or comments that make it easier to break the ice and establish a rapport with the applicant.

Your application form needn't be long or complicated to be effective. In fact, the simpler you can keep it, the better. The important thing is to cover the information that is relevant to a prospective employee's job performance.

In developing the job application form you will be using, keep in mind that federal law prohibits discriminating against anyone on the basis of race, sex, religion, color, or national origin. Nor can you automatically rule out an applicant because of age or because of physical handicap. To stay in compliance with the law, your best bet is to restrict your questions to those that focus on an applicant's ability to do the work.

CONDUCT INTERVIEWS

Interviewing prospective employees gives you the opportunity to find out more about each applicant's employment background, skills, and education. Such additional factors as an applicant's enthusiasm, ability to communicate, poise, and personal appearance can also be evaluated.

APPLICATION FOR EMPLOYMENT

Name _____ Date _____

        (Last)   (First)   (Middle)

Address _____ Telephone _____

Social security number _____ Are you over 18?_____

Job skills: _____

Equipment you can operate:_____

May we contact your present and previous employers? _____

Employment History (Last position first)

From	To	Name & Address	Position	Reason for leaving
1.				
2.				
3.				
4.				

Education

	Name & Address	Major	Degree
High School			
College			
Other			

References

	Name & Address	Telephone	Relationship
1.			
2.			

I understand that if I am employed and any statement is then found to be not true, I may be released immediately.

Signature _____ Date _____

In conducting interviews, you should select a private, comfortable location in which to talk. Trying to carry on a conversation over the sounds of machinery or ringing telephones is counterproductive. You want to put the applicant at ease so that you can gather the information you need. The trick is to get the other person talking. Too many interviewers dominate the conversation themselves, and then when it's time to make an evaluation they have little to go on.

The way to get the most out of interviews is to be ready for them. For a start, review the job application prior to each interview. This will give you some idea of the person you are about to meet. Keep the application with your during the interview as well, so that you can refer to it if needed or make notes on it. Many staffing experts also recommend writing out a few questions in advance. Then, instead of worrying about what to ask next, you can really listen to what's being said. Immediately after the interview is over, jot down your evaluation of the applicant before you forget anything.

Questions You Can and Cannot Ask

These guidelines should help you to avoid asking discriminatory questions. To make sure you are in compliance with the law, contact your state's Department of Fair Employment.

You Can Ask:

Have you ever used another name?

What is your place of residence?

If hired, can you show proof of age?

Are you over 18 years old?

If hired, can you provide verification of your right to work in the United States?

What languages can you speak, read, or write?

What is the name and address of a parent or guardian (if applicant is a minor)?

Do you have any physical condition that would keep you from performing your job?

Have you ever been convicted of a felony?

What skills have you acquired through military service?

What professional organizations do you belong to?

You Cannot Ask:

What is your maiden name?

Do you own or rent your home?

How old are you? Birthdate?

When did you attend school?

Are you a U.S. citizen?

Where were you born? Your parents?

What is your native tongue?

With whom do you live?

Are you married or single? Divorced?

What does your spouse do?

How many children do you have? Their ages?

Have you made provisions for child care?

What race are you? What color?

What is your height and weight?

Do you have any physical disabilities?

Have you ever applied for Workers' Compensation?

What religion are you?

Have you ever been arrested?

When did you serve in the military? What type of discharge do you have?

What organizations or clubs do you belong to?

VERIFY INFORMATION

Even if you're positive that you've found the best person for the job, don't hire anyone yet. Before you do, there's one more step: Verify the information you've been given. Regardless of how favorable a first impression may be, there's no substitute for checking the facts. It's not a matter of doubting your own judgment; it's just good business sense.

In verifying academic information, ask to see an official copy of the applicant's record from each school attended. Dates of attendance, courses taken, and grades received should all appear on the record. To check an applicant's work history, contact previous employers. This can be done by phone, by letter, or in person. In so doing, though, be prepared to take all comments with a grain of salt; former employers sometimes exaggerate a past employee's attributes or failings. Your job is to try to separate the facts from the fiction.

THE HIRING DECISION IS MADE

Congratulations! Having gone through the previous steps, with any luck you're now ready to select the person you want to hire. This is a time to celebrate—but not a time to rest on your laurels. The staffing process continues.

PROVIDE JOB ORIENTATION

Each new employee needs to be made to feel comfortable in your business. Starting a new job is a cause for uncertainty, no matter how terrific the job is. Getting to know co-workers, keeping track of new duties and responsibilities, and attempting to figure out how the organization operates can easily overwhelm a new employee. It takes time to adjust to a new job. It also takes help from you.

The purpose of a job orientation program is to answer as many questions as possible about your business and the new employee's position within it. Right off the bat, the employee should be filled in on the company's policies and regulations as well as the employee's duties and responsibilities, compensation, and benefits.

Many businesses, small as well as large, provide new hires with an employee handbook that contains the information they need to know. While no substitute for personal communication exists, an employee handbook can help to put your business in the proper perspective and to simplify the employee's adjustment. In putting together a handbook don't feel that it has to be a thick volume, complete with pictures and a fancy cover. A few typewritten pages of clearly presented information can generally do the job. Among the subjects you want to cover in detail are:

- The company's history.
- An explanation of the company's products or services.
- Company policies and procedures.
- Employee compensation benefits.

PROVIDE TRAINING

The welfare of both your business and your employees rests on the quality of training that you are able to provide. To carry out their current jobs and to obtain the skills necessary to advance into more challenging jobs, employees need guidance and training. Without it, skills and motivation begin to stagnate and decline, productivity drops off, and the business suffers. All needlessly.

A training program helps employees to grow so that they can help your business grow. Some of the kinds generally utilized are on-the-job training, job rotation, specialized training, and management development.

On-the-job training endeavors to instruct an employee in how to carry out a particular job assignment. Equally useful in training new employees and employees who are changing jobs, it consists of four parts:

1. *Preparation.* The trainer finds out what the employee already knows about the job.
2. *Demonstration.* The trainer shows the employee how to do the job.
3. *Application.* The employee does the job alone.
4. *Inspection.* The work is inspected and suggestions or comments made.

Job rotation allows employees to learn new jobs and broaden their skills by working at different assignments on a temporary basis. As a result, workers become more versatile, tedium is reduced, and scheduling is simplified because of worker flexibility.

Specialized training can enable an employee to hone old skills or master new ones. Through company-offered courses or outside courses at local colleges or trade schools, employees can learn how to operate a new piece of machinery, type faster, improve sales presentations, read a blueprint, or do any number of things beneficial to both the employees and the company.

Management development is geared toward training people to enter management or to advance within the managerial ranks. By means of courses on such subjects as leadership, decision making, planning, and communication, employees can be groomed to accept more responsibility.

EVALUATE PERFORMANCE

Employees need a yardstick by which to measure their performance and progress. This can be supplied in the form of performance evaluation. Conducted at regular intervals, this evaluation should highlight an employee's strengths and pinpoint the areas that need improvement.

One method of evaluation that is popular with employees and employers alike is *management by objectives* (MBO). Its appeal stems from the fact that it contains no surprises or hidden clauses; everything expected of the employee is spelled out in advance as objectives. Furthermore, these objectives are decided upon jointly by the worker and the worker's boss. Together, as a team, they set down on paper the targets that the employee will strive to reach. Later, when it's time to evaluate the employee's performance, it's easy to see which objectives have been met and which ones need additional work. New objectives can then be set and the evaluation process continued.

COMPENSATE EMPLOYEES

To attract and retain high-caliber employees, it's necessary to compensate them at the going wage or better. Trying to get something for nothing just leads to employee dissatisfaction and high turnover. And if your employes feel that you're taking advantage of them, chances are that they'll find a way to take advantage of you. Work slowdowns and theft are just two of the many ways possible.

In addition to comparing favorably with the competition, your policy on wages should be an equitable one that rewards employees on the basis of merit. This instills loyalty and motivates employees to work harder and to expand their skills, so that they can increase their earnings.

Another kind of compensation that employees have come to expect is called *fringe benefits*. These consist of such components as a health plan, pension plan, life insurance, bonuses, and profit sharing. These vary from company to company and may not be applicable or affordable for your business. They should certainly be considered, however.

MONITOR EMPLOYEE TURNOVER

Once an employee quits, who cares what the employee thinks about your business? You do. It's just as important to pay heed to an employee's reason for leaving as it is to listen to a job applicant's reasons for wanting to work for you. This is your chance to find out something about your business that might help you to make it a better place in which to work. Hiring and training employees is costly and time-consuming. Any information associated with reducing turnover is worth listening to.

Before the employee leaves, an *exit interview* should be scheduled. During this interview, the employee should be asked the reasons for leaving (better salary, promotion, dissatisfaction with the job, return to school, spouse's job transfer). The employee's opinions regarding the company, its policies, and its personnel should also be solicited. Your goal isn't to debate the issues or to convince a dissatisfied worker to stay, but to obtain information you can refer to in making future plans. A sample form to use for this interview is provided on page 136.

EXIT INTERVIEW REPORT

1. Name of employee _____

2. Date _____

3. Department _____ 4. Shift_____

5. Date hired _____

6. Address _____

_____

7. Male _____ Female _____ 8. Age _____

9. Marital status _____

10. Education _____

11. Job title or position _____

12. Name of supervisor _____

13. Veteran? _____ 14. Handicap? _____

15. Would you rehire? _____

16. Previous training_____

_____

_____

_____

17. Type of separation

_____

_____

_____

18. Reasons for separation

_____

_____

_____

19. Indirect causes for separation

_____

_____

_____

20. Action taken

_____

_____

_____

STAFFING CHECKLIST

In order to recruit, hire, and retain the best people available for your business, take a moment to answer the questions in the following Staffing Checklist.

	Answer Yes or No
1. Have you analyzed each job that you want filled?	_____
2. Have you prepared job descriptions?	_____
3. Do you know what sources to use in recruiting employees?	_____
4. Will you utilize an application form?	_____
5. Do you know the information that can and cannot be included on an application form?	_____
6. Do you know what to do to prepare for an interview?	_____
7. Will you verify the information received from each applicant that you are seriously considering?	_____
8. Have you decided on the kind of job orientation to give your new employees?	_____
9. Have you prepared an employee handbook?	_____
10. Do you know which form(s) of job training to utilize?	_____
11. Have you determined how often to evaluate your employees?	_____
12. Do you intend to use an evaluation form when evaluating employees?	_____
13. Will your employees be adequately compensated for the work they perform?	_____
14. Are you planning to monitor employee turnover?	_____
15. Will you use an exit interview report?	_____
16. Do you intend to listen to the advice of employees who are leaving and take advantage of worthwhile suggestions?	_____

12

Managing and Motivating

The key to entrepreneurial success is getting others to commit to your vision and to work at making it a reality. Few successful businesses are the result of one person's solo efforts. It isn't enough for an entrepreneur to be good at producing a product or performing a service. If your business is to grow and prosper, you must be a leader.

In addition to finding the best qualified people to work in your business, you need to come up with effective ways to manage and motivate them. Technical skills alone won't do it. Your technical skills can get your business started, but it's your human relations skills that will keep it going.

DEVELOPING YOUR OWN MANAGEMENT STYLE

No one management style is best for everyone. It's a matter of finding a style that you feel comfortable with and that works well in your particular situation. In the broadest sense, there are as many ways to manage as there are managers. Focusing on the most commonly used management styles, though, three become clear: autocratic, democratic, and free-rein.

Autocratic Management

Business owners who use an autocratic management style keep most of the authority to themselves, making decisions without consulting

138

others. More inclined to give orders than to ask for advice, they generally adopt a take-charge approach to management. When the situation calls for fast, decision action, they are ready to move.

The autocratic management style works best in fast-paced, volatile industries where there isn't time to confer with others and in situations where employees are lacking in experience or motivation. The drawback to this style is that it can generate resentment and frustration among workers who feel that their input is being ignored. Furthermore, by making all the decisions alone, entrepreneurs can end up limiting their businesses' growth potential by failing to develop the employee management talent needed to run a larger operation.

Democratic Management

As the name implies, a democratic management style gives employees a much greater say in decision making. Rather than making unilateral decisions and expecting employees to carry them out, the entrepreneur encourages employees to get involved in the process. Business owners who take a *participative* approach to managing delegate authority whenever possible, but retain the final right to approval.

The democratic management style works best with employees who have strong job skills and require only minimum supervision. Among its advantages are the feelings of belonging, pride, and commitment that it can instill in workers and its ability to tap employees' ideas and ingenuity for the good of the business. The main disadvantages of this management style are the time it takes to get employees' input and the weakening or "watering down" of decisions that can occur in reaching a consensus.

Free-Rein Management

A free-rein management style—also called a *laissez-faire* style, from the French expression "leave it alone"—gives employees the most authority of all. Business owners who use this style hire the best workers they can find and let them make the majority of the decisions concerning their job functions and responsibilities. Utilizing a hands-off approach to managing, the entrepreneur sets goals and objectives for the business but leaves employees relatively free to perform their duties as they see fit.

The free-rein management style works best with professionals, such as engineers, scientists, writers, and others, who are expected to function independently. It's often used with outside salespeople who operate in the field and must determine the best ways to manage their time and serve customers' needs. The main weakness of this style is that, by letting employees set their own agendas, workers can end up pursuing their own interests rather than the ones most beneficial to the business.

To find the right management style for you, you should look at three factors:

- Yourself.
- Your employees.
- The work environment.

Looking at yourself. Being a good manager isn't just knowing what makes people tick, but what makes *you* tick. The more you know about yourself, your management abilities, and temperament, the better you will be able to capitalize on your strengths and compensate for your weaknesses. How willing are you to share authority with others? Have you ever managed people before? How many? For how long? In what capacity? What's your approach to problem solving? Are you more comfortable working alone or as part of a team?

Looking at your employees. Just as managers are different, so are the people they manage. Part of choosing a management style involves matching it to the workforce. Are your employees more likely to:

a. Show initiative, work independently without supervision, accept responsibility, be creative problem solvers, take pride in doing their jobs well?

   OR:

b. Avoid work when they can, goof off, wait for someone to "tell" them what to do, cut corners when no one's looking?

In the first instance, less supervision is needed; a management style that gives employees more say in decision making should work well. In the second instance, though, a more authoritarian management style is called for that provides closer supervision and tighter controls.

Looking at the work environment.   The nature of the work being done also plays a big part in determining which management style is most effective. Are your employees performing creative, varied tasks that change from day to day or from one project to the next? Or are they performing repetitive tasks that basically remain the same? Workers that perform varied tasks—scientists in a research lab or an ad agency's creative staff, for example—generally respond best to a management style that offers a high degree of freedom to carry out their respective tasks in the manner they think best. Workers that perform repetitive tasks—such as on an assembly line or processing forms—usually need a management style that is more direction-oriented, clearly stating what needs to be accomplished and when. This isn't to say that their inputs aren't equally valuable or shouldn't be sought out. They should be, but in a more structured way, possibly through *quality circles*—meetings where workers discuss ways to increase productivity and job satisfaction.

Once you've taken these factors into consideration, you should be able to arrive at the management style that provides the best "fit" for your specific business. If you don't hit on it immediately, though, don't get upset or discouraged. Developing a management style takes time, and, once you've found a method that works for you, you have to keep fine tuning it. As people and circumstances change, so does the need for one management style or another.

KNOWING WHEN TO DELEGATE

Unlike corporate managers, who are used to getting things done through people, entrepreneurs often want to do everything themselves. Whichever management style you choose, you must become proficient at delegating authority. Whether you delegate the minimum amount possible (autocratic management) or the maximum amount (free-rein management), there will be times when you have to let someone else make the decision. It's not a question of whether to delegate, but *when*. One person simply can't do it all.

To make the delegation process go smoothly and get positive results, try following these suggestions:

1. Go low.   One of the first rules of management is to delegate authority to the lowest *competent* level in an organization. How low can you go? To the person who has the knowledge, skills, and willingness needed to carry out the job. A clerk may be competent to order office supplies, but you wouldn't expect that person to choose a new site for your business. Pushing decisions down to the lowest competent level possible frees you and any high-level workers in your business to focus your attention on more important matters.

2. *Give enough authority.* The most common mistake in delegating is not giving workers enough authority to carry out their duties and responsibilities. Expecting salespersons to satisfy customers, but not giving them the authority to make exchanges or refunds is an example.

3. *State what's expected.* Let employees know the scope of the work involved and what you want them to accomplish, such as buying merchandise, negotiating a contract, training a new employee.

4. *Be supportive.* Make it clear to employees that they can come to you for help if they need it. Just knowing that you're available to offer advice or information should help to relieve any job anxiety the employee may have.

5. *Keep communication channels open.* The easier it is for employees to communicate with each other and with you, the easier it will be for them to carry out their assignments. Making the information that workers need to have readily accessible not only speeds things up, but helps to keep mistakes from happening.

6. *Establish controls.* Although the act of delegating involves giving up control, it also calls for you to establish controls. "Controls," in this sense, are guidelines or limits within which the work must be performed. For example, telling a supervisor to increase the productivity in his or her department doesn't go far enough. How much should it be increased? Within what time frame?

7. *Create opportunities to succeed.* Rather than setting employees up for failure, set them up for success. By picking the right person for a job and providing the resources (people, time, money, information) needed to succeed, you can develop strong, confident managers capable of making your business thrive.

FINDING WAYS TO MOTIVATE

One of the biggest challenges a business owner can face is finding ways to motivate employees. It would be simple if everyone wanted the same thing from a job and was driven by the same needs. But they aren't. People are different, and what motivates one person may not motivate another.

Identifying Needs

Just as important as the ability to identify your customers' needs is the ability to identify your employees' needs. What's important to them? What needs do they expect to be fulfilled by working for you? The need for money? Achievement? Recognition? Power? Creativity? Interaction with others? Security? Personal satisfaction?

One of the mistakes business owners make is thinking that money is the only motivator. Their common refrain is, "I pay a fair wage. I expect a fair day's work." Then when they don't get it, they wonder why employees are so lazy or don't care about doing a good job anymore.

The thing to realize is that money is just one of many motivators. In some situations it may not even be a motivator. For example, a construction worker who's just put in two months of 60-hour work weeks may be less than thrilled by the prospect of earning additional overtime pay. Instead of being a motivator, the overtime is actually a *de*motivator. What the worker really wants is some time off to spend with family and friends.

You can use a number of motivators to increase workers' productivity. These include offering such incentives as:

- Interesting work.
- Opportunities for advancement.
- Competitive salaries.
- Bonuses.
- Ownership in the business.
- Job training.
- Recognition.
- Responsibility.
- New challenges.
- Fair treatment.

- Good fringe benefits.
- Positive work environment.
- Flexible hours.
- Job security.
- Praise.
- Respect.

The trick, of course, is knowing which incentives to use. Through careful observation and by taking the time to know your employees, you should be able to determine which incentives will work best with which people. For instance, an employee who is in debt or barely making ends meet is obviously going to be more motivated by financial incentives than by the opportunity to make friends on the job. The very opposite could be true, though, for someone who's new in the area or who worked in a business where the employees didn't get along. A person with low self-esteem is likely to respond to praise. A high achiever, who's already doing well, might do even better if given additional responsibilities or a stake in the business.

To be effective, the incentives you offer must meet both the needs of individual employees and of your business. There aren't very many small businesses that can match the salaries and benefits packages offered by major corporations. But they often have other incentives that employees want even more: the chance to be part of a growing business, greater responsibility, enthusiastic co-workers, opportunities for creativity and recognition, or a piece of the pie (through partnerships, stock options, and so on). Rather than just being another cog in the wheel, following long-set policies and procedures, they can have a real impact on your business—if you'll let them.

To make sure that the incentives you use have the desired effect of motivating workers, rather than demotivating them, keep in mind that:

- The incentive must be something that the employee wants. In other words, it must meet some unfulfilled need.
- The incentive must be seen as something positive. If you give an employee additional responsibilities, will that be viewed as a reward for good job performance or as a ploy to get more work done?
- The incentive must be known. Employees must be aware of the incentive before it can motivate them. Praising an employee's work to a business associate, but not to the employee, for example, will not provide any incentive.

- The incentive must be fair. Showing favoritism and rewarding some workers for their accomplishments, but not others, demoralizes employees and divides the workforce.

- The incentive must be attainable. Setting a sales quota needed to qualify for a bonus beyond employees' reach will have a reverse effect, causing them to cut back, rather than increase, their sales efforts.

- The incentive must change as workers needs change. Once a need is fulfilled, it no longer is a motivator. An employee whose primary motivation was money is likely to want other things—recognition, personal satisfaction—once the need for financial security has been met.

Sharing Your Vision

The best way of all to motivate employees is by sharing your vision for the business with them and showing how your success relates to their success. You need to make employees feel that they have a vested interest in the business, that it's theirs too, and that the work they do is important.

To share your vision, you must be able to put it into words and communicate it to others. Every employee should know what your business stands for, what it hopes to accomplish, and the rewards to be earned by contributing to its success.

Only when employees see that the business's future is interlocked with their own will they be willing to fully commit to your vision and to do the things necessary to enable you to achieve it.

LEADERSHIP CHECKLIST

To evaluate your leadership skills and determine if you are effectively managing and motivating your employees, answer the questions in the following Leadership Checklist.

	Answer Yes or No

1. Do you know the strengths and weaknesses of the three most common management styles?
   Autocratic
   Democratic
   Free-rein
	_____
	_____
	_____

2. In evaluating each style have you considered the major factors affecting your business?
   Your own abilities/preferences
   Your employees
   The work environment
	_____
	_____
	_____

3. Have you chosen the management style that's best for you?	_____
4. Have you given thought to the responsibilities and authority that you're willing to delegate?	_____
5. Are you familiar with how the delegation process works?	_____
6. Have you identified the various needs of your employees?	_____
7. Have you determined the types of incentives that you want to use?	_____
8. Do you know which incentives will be the most effective at motivating which workers?	_____
9. Do you know how to keep incentives from having a reverse effect and becoming demotivators?	_____
10. Can you put your vision for your business into words?	_____
11. Are you ready to share your vision with others?	_____
12. Will helping you to achieve your goals enable employees to achieve their own goals as well?	_____

13

Developing Your Promotional Strategy

If you build a better mousetrap, the world may indeed beat a path to your door. But not without a little help from you. In the first place, before people can buy your mousetrap, they have to know about it. In the second place, they have to know where to find your door. In the third place, it helps if the people you're trying to reach are having trouble with rodents.

The U.S. Patent Office has issued patents by the thousands for inventions that never made it. Putting aside the problems of unworkable designs or excessive production costs, many of the inventions failed simply because of poor or nonexistent promotional strategies. Having created their better mousetraps, the inventors didn't know what to do with them.

Forming a business is much the same as inventing a new product. To succeed, each needs to be promoted. Having answered the questions in Chapters 2 and 3 on planning and determining the best location, you've already evaluated the need for your particular product or service. And you have a pretty good idea who your potential customers are. Knowing this much is half the battle. Now, what's left is to convert those potential customers into satisfied customers. That's where your promotional strategy comes in.

A promotional strategy is a game plan for reaching your target market—those people most likely to use your product or service. At the simplest, most direct level, your promotional strategy might consist of relying on a sign in front of your door and the word-of-mouth

comments of your present customers. In some instances—if you're
in a very small town, or if you offer unique products or services, or
if you have a long-standing reputation, for example—this is sufficient. Normally, though, customers need more to go on before they
are drawn to your business.

The goal of your promotional strategy should be to reach the
greatest number of potential customers through the most economical use of your resources (money, personnel, and facilities). This entails tuning in to those channels of communication (by means of
advertising and publicity) most widely used by your target customers. It also entails working within the limits of a budget to
achieve the desired results.

ADVERTISING

Advertising involves the purchasing of time or space in the various
communications media for the purpose of promoting your business.
The two categories of advertising are institutional and product. *Institutional advertising* promotes your business in general, emphasizing its good name and any contributions that it has made to the
well-being of the community. *Product advertising* promotes the
specific products or services you sell, emphasizing the benefits associated with buying them from you. An oil company, for instance,
can emphasize the time and money it spends in exploring for new
sources of fuel (institutional advertising), or it can emphasize the
special additives that make its gasoline better than the rest (product
advertising). Your own objectives will determine whether to use one
or both of these approaches.

THE MEDIA

The advertising media generally favored are newspapers, magazines, radio, television, direct mail, *Yellow Pages*, and outdoor advertising. Other media include transit, specialty, movie theaters, flyers,
church bulletins, and sponsoring sporting teams.

Each medium has its own unique characteristics and is capable
of reaching large numbers of people. Depending on your message,
target customers, budget, and lead time, some will be more suited to
your needs than others.

First of all, is your *message* simple and direct ("You'll save more
money at Jones's Hardware Store"), or is it more complicated, in-
volving a detailed explanation (a listing of the nutrients in your spe-

cial health food drink)? Does your message rely heavily on words, color, sound, or movement to make its point?

Second, is your *target customer* everyone (the mass market) or just a small segment of the market? The narrower your target, the greater the need to use selective media to reach it. Doctors, for instance, can be reached more effectively by means of a medical journal than a daytime soap opera.

Third, consider your *budget*. How much money can you spend? Despite the suitability of a particular medium, if you can't afford it there's no sense in building your promotional strategy around it.

Finally, what is your *lead time*? Do you want the advertisement to start this week, next month, next year? Lead times vary with the medium, and if you need a quick start, that limits your selection.

Newspapers

Newspapers, which have traditionally been the favorite means of advertising for retailers, account for more than a fourth of all advertising dollars spent in the United States.

Message. Newspapers are one of the best equipped of the media (along with magazines and direct mail) for explaining and describing a product. Not only is the space available, but the only limitation on time is the reader's attention span. The effectiveness of your message can be quickly and easily measured through the use of redeemable coupons in your ads and customer demand for the featured items. If no one brings in a coupon or asks for the product, the ad isn't working.

Target customer. Since newspapers are local, they reach the people in your own community. Their readers are your potential customers. For greater selectivity, your ad can be placed in the sections most likely to appeal to your target customer (sports, business, world news, entertainment, food, real estate). An ad for a restaurant might run in either the entertainment or the food section.

Budget. Newspaper rates are low compared to most other media. Even a business on a very limited budget can generally afford a small ad.

Lead time. Newspapers have the shortest lead time of the media. Some ads can be placed on as little as two or three days' notice. This gives you a great deal of flexibility in deciding when and what to advertise.

Limitations. Newspapers are short-lived; if your ad isn't read today, chances are that it won't ever be read. Reproduction quality is poor; products that require strong visual presentations are better served by other media. Most people don't read every page in a newspaper; unless careful attention is paid to your ad's placement, it could get lost in the shuffle.

Rates. Advertising space is sold in column inches (14 lines to an inch). An ad that's 2 columns wide by 3 inches deep occupies 6 column inches. The rate per column inch is based on a paper's circulation: the larger the circulation, the higher the rates.

Volume rates. Bigger advertisers are entitled to discounts. This means that the more space you buy, the lower the rate per column inch.

Preferred position rates. If you specify a particular position, page, or position on the page, the rate is higher. But if this gets people to see your ad, it's worth the money. Because of the way we read, ads at the upper right of the page generally have the most drawing power.

Classified rates. These rates are quoted by lines, rather than column inches. The ideal position is at the front of the classified section. The farther back that your ad appears, the larger the drop-off in readers.

Comparing costs. Depending on your location, there may be several newspapers to choose from. Based on each paper's rates and circulation, it's an easy matter to compare the costs and determine which is the best buy. This is done by measuring each paper's cost per thousand people reached, or CPM.

$$CPM = \frac{Cost\ of\ ad \times 1,000}{Total\ circulation}$$

$$CPM = \frac{\$500 \times 1,000}{650,000} = 77¢ \text{ per 1,000 for newspaper A}$$

$$CPM = \frac{\$460 \times 1,000}{575,000} = 80¢ \text{ per 1,000 for newspaper B}$$

As you can see, although an ad in newspaper A is more expensive, its cost per thousand readers is actually less. This makes it the better buy.

Magazines

Though used primarily by large advertisers, magazines are now starting to grow in popularity with smaller advertisers as well. This is because of the increase in special-interest magazines. Unlike general-interest magazines, these focus on a single topic (films, needlepoint, travel, skiing, gardening) and enable advertisers to reach a specific audience.

Message. Like newspapers, magazines are well suited to conveying in-depth information, and their effectiveness can be readily measured. Reproduction values are high; so products that need color or strong visuals to make an impact look their best. Furthermore, people tend to read magazines at a more leisurely pace than newspapers and are inclined to save them afterward. This lengthens the lifespan of your ad.

Target customer. Magazines enable you to be as selective as you want in pinpointing your target customer. Through careful placement of your ads in the right special-interest magazines, you're virtually guaranteed of reaching a receptive audience.

Budget. Magazine ads can be expensive, particularly in national magazines with large circulations. But if you're willing to do some research, there are bargains to be found. For information about rates check the *Standard Rate and Data Service*, a monthly publication available at many libraries.

Lead time. Magazines have a much longer lead time than newspapers. Ads normally must be received two or three months prior to publication.

Limitations. The long lead time reduces your flexibility; ads must be planned and space purchased well in advance. Magazine ads can get lost too; position is important.

Rates. Space is usually sold by the page or fraction of a page. Some magazines also have classified or mail order sections in which space is sold by the line. These sections are generally at the back of the magazines. Rates are determined by circulation. However, a magazine that caters to a particularly affluent or hard-to-reach audience may still be able to charge high rates despite a small circulation. Other determinants of rates are:

- Color. An ad that's in color is more expensive than a black-and-white ad.
- Quantity discounts. These are based on the amount of space purchased in a 12-month period.
- Frequency discounts. These are based on the number of times space is purchased in a 12-month period.
- Positioning. If a special position is requested, there is an additional charge.

Comparing costs. As with newspapers, magazines can be compared by the CPM technique to determine which is the most economical.

Radio

Radio's main strength is its ability to reach people regardless of where they are or what they're doing. Whether at home, driving to work, or on vacation, people have their radios with them. In the United States today there are almost two radios per person, with 99 percent of all households having at least one radio.

Message. Radio uses words, music, and sound effects to communicate its message. It has strong emotional impact, which is derived from its ability to establish a rapport with the audience and move listeners to action. Jingles and slogans are common in radio commercials because listeners remember them later. This helps to reinforce brand identification.

Target customer. Radio stations, like special-interest magazines, gear themselves toward a particular audience. Through the program format you select (top 40 rock music, country music, classical music, middle of the road, easy listening, talk show, news), it's possible to zero in on your target customer.

Budget. The cost of purchasing air time depends on a program's popularity and the frequency of your commercials. To determine costs, check the *Standard Rate and Data Service.*

Lead time.   Lead times vary. Certain programs may be booked as much as a year in advance, while others have immediate openings.

Limitations.   Many radio stations are competing for audiences; this may make it necessary to buy time on a number of stations to reach all your target customers. To be effective at all, your commercial needs to be broadcast more than once; this repetition increases your costs. The lifespan of your commercial is just seconds; unlike a print advertisement, it gets only one chance to communicate your message. Radio is a medium without visuals; if your product has to be seen to be believed you're wasting your money.

Rates.   Time is sold in units of 60 seconds or less— that is, in 10-, 15-, 30-, and 60-second spots. Although 60-second commercials once dominated the airwaves, the trend is now toward shorter ones, with 30-second spots currently the most popular.

Rates are based on both a station's coverage and its circulation. *Coverage* is the geographical area covered by the station's signal. *Circulation* refers to the potential number of listeners in the area. Since the number of listeners can vary throughout the day, different rates are charged for different time periods.

Drive time.   This is the most expensive time of day because it covers the intervals from 6 to 10 A.M. and from 4 to 7 P.M., when people are in their cars driving to and from work.

Run-of-the-station (ROS).   This is the cheapest time because it allows the station to put your commercial anywhere it pleases.

Weekly plan.   A weekly plan offers a lower rate to advertisers purchasing a package of time. Each package contains a variety of time slots, ranging from drive time to ROS.

Comparing costs.   Stations can be compared by means of the cost-per-thousand technique.

Television

Though television trails newspapers as the most picked advertising medium, it is rapidly closing in on the top spot. The reason for television's growing popularity is simple: numbers. Currently 98 percent of all American households have one or more television sets, and the average family watches for more than six hours per day. The newest of the media, television's impact on its audience is still being explored. But the fact that it can shape attitudes and change opinions is already known.

Message. Television is the most intimate of the media; combining sight, sound, color, and motion, it takes your presentation right into the viewer's home. Television lets you show off your product, rather than just tell about it. The viewer sees it in a natural setting that encourages acceptance. (If the people in the commercial are satisfied with the product, why shouldn't the viewer be too?)

Target customer. More than any of the other media, television is a mass medium. At any one time, millions of viewers are watching. Programs like the Super Bowl, the World Series, and the Academy Awards Ceremony are tuned in by viewers worldwide. The question is: Are these your target customers? In selecting a program on which to advertise, it's as important to check the data describing the viewers (age, sex, income, interests) as it is to check the number of people who are watching.

Budget. Unfortunately, advertising on television is expensive. Regardless of its appeal, the majority of small businesses will find it beyond their budgets. However, local and cable television stations offer considerably reduced rates, and these may be a viable alternative. For further information, check the *Standard Rate and Data Service.*

Lead time. Top-rated television shows are likely to be booked a year in advance. Time slots on less popular shows and new shows are generally available on a few days' notice.

Limitations. Television has less selectivity than the other media; using it to reach a small target audience could be an exercise in overkill. Viewers often leave the room during commercials; getting and holding their attention isn't easy. Television commercials, like radio commercials, become more effective with repetition; this adds to your cost.

Rates. Time is sold in units of 60 seconds or less, with 30-second spots currently the most favored. Rates vary on the basis of the time period selected and the size of the audience for a given program—hence the importance of the Nielsen and Arbitron ratings, which rank programs in the order of their popularity.

Prime time. This is the most costly time. It covers the hours from 7 to 11 P.M., when the greatest number of viewers are watching television.

Discounts. These are available on essentially the same terms as those offered by radio stations.

Comparing costs. The CPM technique applies.

Direct Mail

Direct mail refers to any printed material of a promotional nature, that is mailed directly to the intended customer—brochures, letters, price lists, catalogs, coupons. This is currently the third most popular choice with advertisers and is used by the majority of businesses, large and small.

Message. Like newspapers and magazines, direct mail is one of the best formats for conveying in-depth information. It also offers the greatest flexibility, since any message can be sent to anyone at any time. Direct mail is regularly used to:

- Inform customers of sales.
- Introduce new products.
- Announce price changes.
- Solicit mail order business.
- Solicit phone order business.
- Maintain customer contact.
- Reach new customers.
- Develop your image.

Target customers. The success of a direct mail campaign is primarily determined by the mailing list. Unless your mailing is going out to the people who are likely to buy your product, you're wasting both time and money. How can you obtain a mailing list that's right for you? You can either purchase it from someone else or build your own list. There are a number of companies in the business of compiling and selling mailing lists. These lists are available in literally thousands of categories (women between the ages of 18 and 45, teenagers, skiers, photography enthusiasts, recent graduates, cooking enthusiasts). Regardless of your target market, there is probably an applicable list. The cost may be as low as $12 per thousand names or as high as $300 per thousand.

If you prefer to build your own list, some of the sources you may be able to use are:

- Your own customers.
- Telephone directories.
- Professional, trade, and industrial directories.
- Credit bureaus.
- Newspaper announcements (wedding, graduation, birth, new business).
- Construction permits on file in municipal and county offices.

Budget. Direct mail's flexibility makes it possible to structure a campaign to meet practically any budget. You should consider:

- The cost of the mailing list.
- The cost of the package (printed materials).
- The cost of postage.
- The cost of labor (addressing, stuffing, and sealing envelopes).

The more extensive the mail, the higher the cost.

Lead time. You control the lead time.

Limitations. In terms of unit costs, direct mail is expensive; it has the highest cost per thousand of the media. There's only a fine line between direct mail and junk mail; make sure you are sending your mailing to the people who really want it.

Rates. Since there is no space or time to be purchased, there are no set rates to consider.

Yellow Pages

Adding to the appeal of *Yellow Pages* advertising is the growing number of specialty directories from which to choose: *The Neighborhood Directory, Silver Pages, Business to Business Directory,* and so on.

Message. A *Yellow Pages* display ad is an attention-getting device. Since your ad is surrounded by those of your competition, it's important that you focus in on the best way to differentiate yourself from the rest—lowest prices, widest selection, friendly service, or whatever.

Target customer. The main advantage of *Yellow Pages* advertising is its ability to reach your target customer at the time they want to buy. Thus your audience is presold. Having already decided *what* to buy, customers are just looking for the right *place* to buy it.

Budget. *Yellow Pages* ads are inexpensive in comparison to the other media.

Lead time. Your ad must be placed before the closing date for inclusion in the current directory.

Limitations. You can't make changes in your ad; it runs as is until the next directory printing.

Rates. Any business with a phone is entitled to a one-line listing, free of charge. To find out the rates for display ads, contact your local *Yellow Pages* sales representative.

Outdoor Advertising

Outdoor advertising involves the use of signs, posters, and billboards to promote your business. In the simplest sense, it can serve as a marker identifying your location. In the broadest sense, it can create an image, getting people to think of your name whenever they think of a particular product.

Message. Your message needs to be simple and direct. Concise copy, bold graphics, and a recognizable product are essential. Remember, the average passerby spends less than 10 seconds reading your ad.

Target customer. Although outdoor advertising is visible to anyone who cares to look, a fairly high degree of selectivity can be achieved through the geographic placement of your advertisement. For instance, ads for airlines, hotels, restaurants, shops, and tourist attractions are typically found on billboards near airports and along freeways where travelers can see them.

Budget. The costs of outdoor advertising are among the lowest of the media.

Lead time. If you're just using signs at your place of business, the only lead time is the production and installation time. In the case of posters and billboards, space is rented on an availability basis and there may be a waiting list for the locations you want.

Limitations. Your advertisement is competing with numerous others; its effectiveness hinges on its ability to command attention. Some people regard outdoor advertising as a form of visual pollution; part of the response to your ads may thus be negative.

Rates. The rates charged for posters and billboards are based on the size and location of the space being leased. Locations are classified by territories, which are priced according to traffic counts. The higher the count, the higher the cost.

Comparing costs. The CPM technique can be used to compare territories to determine the most economical purchase.

Other Advertising Media

Some of the other forms of advertising you may wish to consider are:

- Transit advertising. Messages are displayed on the exteriors and interiors of trains, buses, and taxicabs.
- Specialty advertising. Your company's name or logo imprinted on such items as calendars, memo pads, book markers, ashtrays, matches, key chains, and T-shirts.
- Flyers. These can be handed out to passers-by or placed on automobile windshields.
- Theater screen advertising. Ads are shown during intermissions.

PUBLICITY

In addition to advertising, you can use publicity to promote your business. This involves getting information about your company's activities or products reported in the news media. Such coverage is provided when the information is thought to have news value or to be of interest to the public.

Although publicity and advertising are similar, they differ in three vital areas: *cost, control,* and *credibility.* Publicity is free. There is no cost to you for the media coverage you receive. Nor do you have any control over that coverage. Unlike advertising, publicity can be favorable or unfavorable—as likely to point out your business's flaws as its accomplishments. If a news broadcast chooses to focus on a lawsuit that's been brought against you, rather than on your volunteer service to the community, there's nothing you can do about it. This very lack of control is what gives publicity its greatest strength—credibility. The fact that it's the news media, rather than a sponsor, delivering your message makes it more believable than advertising.

While it's impossible to control the publicity you get, it *is* possible to influence it. The way to do this is by maintaining good press relations, providing timely and accurate information in the form of press releases, pointing out the angle that makes your story interesting or newsworthy, being available to answer questions, and not making unreasonable demands. By learning to work within the limitations of publicity, you can put yourself in a position to take full advantage of it.

Press Releases

Far from being anything mysterious, a press release is simply a fact sheet. Explaining who, what, where, when, and how, it states the details of the story you want the press to tell. It also makes the reporter's job easier by emphasizing *why* your story will be of interest to the public. Possible "why's" include:

- Having a unique product or service.
- Staging a special event.
- Helping a charity.
- Winning an award.
- Giving a speech.

This story angle—or *hook,* as it is called—is the most important information of all, helping to justify your story to the media and to shape the coverage you receive.

PRESS RELEASE FORMAT

Business Name
Address

Contact: Your Name
Phone Number

Release Date (For Immediate Release; For Release after October 20, etc.):

Start copy here and begin with your angle: Why

Provide all necessary details: Who
What
Where
When
How

Write in short, clear sentences and paragraphs.
  Two pages should be the maximum length.

Double-space, using one-inch margins on all sides.

Put your name and phone number on each page.

Type "-30-" after the last line of copy to indicate the end. This is a symbol commonly used by printers.

To give your press releases a professional look, use the format shown on this page. In so doing, though, don't make the mistake of cramming too much information into one press release. If you find yourself writing a book or trying to tell two stories at once, the situation probably calls for more than one press release or for a *media kit*.

Although a media kit sounds elaborate and expensive, it needn't be. All it takes is a standard-size folder with two inside pockets. Then, depending on the information you want to send out, you can fill it with such materials as:

- The press release(s).
- A business fact sheet/history.
- A list of suppliers and/or customers.
- A brochure.
- Photographs (5x7, black and white).

PREPARING AN ADVERTISING BUDGET

In preparing their advertising budgets, the majority of businesses base their allocations on a percentage of annual past sales, estimated

SAMPLE ADVERTISING BUDGET

CAMERA SHOP BUDGET

Sales for 19XX	$300,000	
Ad budget as percent of sales	4%	
Total ad budget	$ 12,000	
Direct mail		$ 5,400
Handouts		1,200
Yellow Pages (one payment)		1,440
Newspapers		3,960
Total ad budget		$12,000
Best selling days		
Christmas		
Graduation		
Summer		

BREAKDOWN BY MONTH

Month	Direct mail	Handouts	*Yellow Pages*	Newspapers	Total
January				$ 330	$ 330
February				330	330
March	$ 650			330	980
April				330	330
May	1,350			330	1,680
June		$ 600		330	930
July	1,350			330	1,680
August				330	330
September			$1,440	330	1,770
October				330	330
November	700			330	1,030
December	1,350	600		330	2,280
Total	$5,400	$1,299	$1,440	$3,960	$12,000

sales, or a combination of these. For example, 4 percent of $300,00 in sales equals an advertising budget of $12,000. Some of the reasons for this method's general acceptance are that it gives you more to go on than guesswork, it emphasizes the relationship between advertising and sales, and it's easy to use.

In determining the percent of sales you want to invest in advertising, you should consider your business's needs, the competition, and the economic environment. To find out what similar businesses are spending, it's a good idea to check such sources as trade journals and the reports published by Dun & Bradstreet, Robert Morris Associates, the Accounting Corporation of America, Census Bureau, and Internal Revenue Service. You can find some examples in the chart of typical ad budgets on the following page.

Once you have calculated your budget, the next step is to allocate it over the coming year, indicating the amount to be spent each month and the media to receive it. Keep in mind that some months will require greater expenditures than others. Also, don't forget to plan for any sales or special events you wish to promote. See the sample advertising budget on page 161 to see how this works.

ADVERTISING FOR SMALL BUSINESSES

Category	Typical Ad Budget as Percent of Sales	Media Selected
Apparel stores	2.5–3.5	Direct mail, newspapers, radio
Auto supply shops	1.0–2.0	Direct mail, fliers, newspapers, *Yellow Pages*
Bars and grills	1.0–1.5	Magazines, newspapers, *Yellow Pages*
Beauty salons	2.5–4.0	Direct mail, newspapers, *Yellow Pages*
Book stores	1.8–2.2	Newspapers, *Yellow Pages*
Cafeterias	2.0–2.6	Newspapers, radio, *Yellow Pages*
Catering services	2.0–3.0	Direct mail, fliers, *Yellow Pages*
Dry cleaners	1.2–1.7	Direct mail, fliers, newspapers, *Yellow Pages*
Fabric stores	1.0–2.5	Newspapers, *Yellow Pages*
Flower shops	1.0–2.0	Newspapers, radio, *Yellow Pages*
Gift shops	2.0–2.5	Magazines, newspapers, radio, *Yellow Pages*
Graphic arts specialists	0.5–1.5	Direct mail, magazines, newspapers, *Yellow Pages*
Health clubs	3.0–5.0	Direct mail, newspapers, radio, television, *Yellow Pages*
Ice cream parlors	1.0–2.5	Newspapes, radio, *Yellow Pages*
Jewelry stores	2.5–3.5	Direct mail, magazines, radio, television, *Yellow Pages*
Locksmiths	0.5–1.5	Direct mail, transit, *Yellow Pages*
Mail order	18.0–30.0	Direct mail, magazines, newspapers, television
Photography stores	2.5–4.0	Direct mail, magazines, newspapers, radio, *Yellow Pages*
Sporting goods stores	2.0–2.5	Newspapers, radio, television, *Yellow Pages*
Stationery stores	2.0–3.0	Newspapers, *Yellow Pages*
Ticket agencies	3.0–5.0	Magazines, newspapers, radio, *Yellow Pages*
TV and appliance stores	1.5–2.5	Newspapers, radio, television, *Yellow Pages*
Upholsterers	0.2–0.8	Shopping guides, *Yellow Pages*
Wedding consultants	1.5–2.5	Direct mail, magazines, *Yellow Pages*

PROMOTIONAL STRATEGY CHECKLIST

To help launch your promotional campaign and reach your target market in the most economical way possible, answer the questions in the following Promotional Strategy Checklist.

	Answer Yes or No
1. Do you know who your potential customers are?	_____
2. Have you established a game plan for reaching your target market?	_____
3. Do you know the difference between institutional and product advertising?	_____
4. Do you know the benefits and limitations of each of the following media?	
Newspaper	_____
Magazines	_____
Radio	_____
Television	_____
Direct mail	_____
Yellow Pages	_____
Outdoor advertising	_____
5. Can you compare costs between like forms of advertising (CPM)?	_____
6. Do you know the rates of the different media?	_____
7. Do you know the difference between advertising and publicity?	_____
8. Do you know how to maintain good press relations?	_____
9. Have you prepared an advertising budget?	_____
10. Have you determined which are the best advertising media for your business?	_____
11. Do you know what media are being used by the competition?	_____
12. Do you keep track of competitors' advertising campaigns?	_____
13. Do you know the best times to advertise during the year?	_____

14

Selling and Servicing

Your first priority as a business owner should be to please the customer. Far more important than any single sale that you make is your ability to meet customers' needs and to establish long-term relationships that will keep customers coming back again and again.

Businesses that are more interested in "moving the goods" than in giving customers what they really need and want usually don't last very long. To go the distance, your personal selling and customer service efforts must be directed at satisfying each customer.

A POSITIVE APPROACH TO SELLING

Personal selling involves more than just giving a sales presentation and writing up the order. Today's top salespeople—the kind you want to be or to have in your business—are problem solvers. Equally good at listening as talking, they are able to correctly identify customers' needs and match them to the products or services they sell. Rather than assuming what customers want or pushing the products they want to sell, the best salespeople find out what customers *do* want and then show them how they can have it.

The Selling Process

Like any skill, personal selling entails a set of steps, which when combined results in a successful outcome—in this case, a satisfied customer. As shown here, there are six steps in the selling process. What you and your salespeople do at each step will directly affect your ability to make individual sales, to get repeat sales and referrals, and to build a positive image.

Prospecting

Many sales experts consider this to be the most important step of all: the search for potential customers, or "prospects," to whom you can sell your products or services. In developing a list of prospects (through customer referrals, contacts, market research, mailing lists, and so on), your goal is to focus your attention on those who can be considered *good prospects*. Beyond being able to use your product, a

THE SIX STEPS IN THE SELLING PROCESS

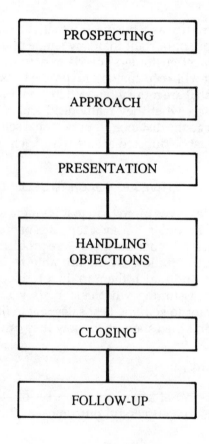

good prospect also (1) has a need for it, (2) can afford it, and (3) is authorized to buy it.

Whether prospecting is something you do alone or you have salespeople involved as well, it must be done. Good prospects are the lifeblood of any business. To expand your customer base and raise sales revenues, you need to actively seek out new customers.

Approach

This step calls for you to make initial contact with the prospect. Your main concern at this point isn't to make an immediate sale, but rather to open up a dialogue with the prospect and to begin to assess his or her needs. During this step what you say, how you dress, and how you act can either work for you or against you. Everything from your greeting, tone of voice, body language, demeanor, and attire should be directed at creating a positive image. As the saying goes, "You don't get a second chance to make a good first impression."

Presentation

Successful sales presentations don't just happen; they are *planned*. Instead of "winging it" or relying on fast talking and fancy footwork to get through sales presentations, the best salespersons plan their presentations carefully. This doesn't mean that you should memorize each word—"canned" presentations tend to come off as stilted and one-sided—but rather that you should think about what the customer's needs are, what points you'd like to make, and what visual aids or demonstration techniques to use.

In planning your presentation, your goals should be to *inform* and *persuade* so that the customer understands what you have to offer and is inclined to buy. Here it helps to do the following:

- Outline the various points you want to make and the order in which to present them.
- Determine how much time you will need (keeping your presentation as concise and to the point as possible).
- Practice your presentation several times until it comes naturally.
- Prepare for different responses so that, as you and the customer interact, you're able to "go with the flow."

Two-way communication. During the presentation itself the most important thing to remember is that communication is a two-way street. In addition to telling the customer things, you must also tune in to what the customer is telling *you*. Is the prospect's response positive or negative? Rather than just steamrolling ahead, you must become adept at recognizing both the *verbal* and *nonverbal* messages the prospect is sending you. Is the person asking questions? If so, that could either be a sign of interest or a defense mechanism to avoid having to make a purchase decision. Is the person leaning in to hear more (generally a good sign) or backing away?

The five senses. Throughout the presentation you should also appeal to the prospect's five senses: the ability to hear, see, touch, smell, and taste. The more senses you can appeal to, the stronger your presentation will be. Rather than just telling how well a car handles, get the prospect to "test drive" it. In the case of a computer, for example, have the prospect sit down and actually use it. Food-related products and services especially lend themselves to this, as prospects find out firsthand how good something looks, smells, and tastes. With some ingenuity, even an intangible product like insurance can be made to appeal to the senses. For example, you could show prospects photographs or a video of smiling policyholders whose insurance policies got them through their misfortunes.

Benefits versus features. Another way to strengthen your sales presentations is by emphasizing benefits rather than features. Whereas features merely describe a product or service, benefits are the *advantages* the prospect will derive from the purchase. As you can see from these examples, the essential difference is that benefits give the prospect a *reason to buy*:

Features	Benefits
This computer program is "user-friendly."	You can start using the program immediately.
These skin products contain special moisturizers.	You'll look younger.
These toys are recommended by educators.	Your child will do better in school.
This ski parka is down-filled.	This parka will keep you warm on the ski slopes.

Converting features into benefits in this way can significantly increase sales. By shifting your focus from what a product or service is to what it can *do* for customers, you enable prospects to more easily envision themselves using it.

Handling Objections

Nice as it would be to conclude each sales presentation by having the customer say, "Yes, I'll take it," that isn't going to happen. You must be prepared for objections. Instead of taking them personally or letting them upset you, just accept the fact that objections come with the territory. Everyone in sales encounters them at one time or another. Many sales professionals go so far as to insist that "the selling doesn't start until the customer says no."

What separates the successful sellers from those who aren't is how they handle the objections. To turn objections into orders, try following these suggestions:

1. **Don't get angry or defensive.** This will just turn the prospect against you and force an end to the sales dialogue.
2. **Deflect the objection in a positive way.** For example, if a prospect thinks your price is too high, you can either point out that it is comparable to competitors', if that's the case, or explain why it's higher—because you offer better quality, have better service, provide a warranty, and so on.
3. **Ask the prospect to restate the objection.** Sometimes when you ask the prospect to restate or explain the objection, you get lucky and the prospect deflects it for you. Or the prospect gives you the information to deflect it yourself. For example, "Well, I really wanted a car that's sportier than that." This gives you the opportunity to show the prospect the two-door version of the car or to show a different model.
4. **Question the objection.** As politely as you can, question the objection that has been raised. Your goal isn't to be confrontational, but rather to determine if the stated objection is indeed the real objection. For example, instead of saying that something is too expensive, a prospect will often raise another objection to avoid making a purchase. If the price (or some other factor) is the real reason, then you can address it: "We have financing available." Or, "You can use our installment plan, if you like."
5. **Shift the prospect's focus.** Ignore the objection, if you can, and shift the prospect's attention to some other aspect of your product or service that you think will be particularly appealing. For example, if a prospect comments that a house you're showing is small, you

might answer, "Yes, it requires very little upkeep." Or, "But look at that view!"

6. **Keep the prospect talking.** The most important thing of all is to keep your dialogue with the prospect going. This gives you the opportunity to do more *probing*—asking questions that enable you to learn more about the prospect's true needs and individual circumstances.

In handling objections, you must also keep in mind that you won't be able to overcome each and every objection. It may be that, for whatever reason (price, style, size, color, fit, purpose, timing, or something else), your product or service *isn't* right for the prospect. In that case not only will it be difficult to make the sale, but you *shouldn't* make it. Even if you could convince the prospect to buy, it wouldn't be in his or her best interest—or in yours. Rather than create a dissatisfied customer, you're better off foregoing the sale and trying for the next best thing: a referral.

Closing

Once you've gotten past any objections, you must be able to do one more thing: close. This is the moment of truth, when you ask the prospect to buy. This step should be a natural extension of the dialogue you've been having with the prospect. Unfortunately, it's a step that many business owners are reluctant to take because they fear rejection. Instead, they just let their sales presentation trail off into nothing, hoping the customer will *ask* to buy. Or they end up saying something like, "Well that's it. If you need any more information, just ask." That's very nice and it may be a good fall-back position to take later. But it *isn't* a close, and it's not likely to result in a sale.

Ways to close. You can close in a number of ways. The simplest and most direct method is to *ask for the order*: "Shall I go ahead and write that up for you now?" This method can get fast results. The main problem with it, though, is that, by asking what's known as a *yes/no* question, you may be setting yourself up for the no.

One way to avoid asking a yes/no question is to *assume the order*. Rather than asking the prospect to buy, you can simply assume the sale has been made and proceed accordingly: "If you'll just fill in this information, I'll finish writing up your order." This method works fine *if* the prospect goes along with you. If the prospect doesn't, then be prepared to ask more questions to keep the dialogue going and try for a second close.

Another popular (and effective) close is the *alternative close*. This avoids the problem of the yes/no question by asking the prospect to choose between two or more alternatives: "Would you prefer the blue or the green?" Or, "Which day would you like it delivered, Monday or Tuesday?" The beauty of this closing technique is that, if the prospect picks one of the choices, the sale is made.

Two other closes you might use are the *added-inducement close* and the *warning-to-buy close*. The first one offers a price reduction, free service, gift, or some other inducement if the prospect buys now: "If you place your order today, I'll pay the shipping charges." The second close warns the prospect to buy before it's too late: "These are the last ones I have in stock. To guarantee delivery, I need to receive your order today." Both closes, while effective, should be used sparingly. The added inducement close cuts into your profit margins and the warning to buy close, if used too often, can be perceived as a high-pressure tactic.

These and other closing methods that you may decide to use can help you to make more sales. Again, it's important to remember, though, that you don't want to force customers into buying what they don't want. The purpose of a close is to make it easy for prospects to choose what's right for them.

Follow-up

The selling process doesn't stop when the sale is made. To keep the customer happy and to ensure yourself of repeat sales and referrals, you must do everything possible to see that the customer is satisfied with the purchase. In a sense this last step is the *first*, offering you the opportunity to reestablish contact with the customer and to begin the selling process again.

MAINTAINING GOOD CUSTOMER RELATIONS

Considering the time and money that go into finding prospects and convincing them to buy, it makes sense to maintain good customer relations. After all, it's easier to sell to a customer who's already sold on your business than it is to sell to someone who doesn't know anything about you. This explains why so many businesses claim that, "After the sale we don't forget the service."

To make sure that your customers are getting the service they deserve, it's important for you to do the following:

- Expedite each purchase.
- Provide personal service.
- Answer questions.
- Handle complaints.
- Solve problems.
- Stay in touch.

Expedite the Purchase

Nothing is more frustrating to a customer than deciding to buy something and then having to wait longer than necessary to receive it. As the seller, you want to make certain that there are no delays in getting your product or service to the customer. Once the sale is made, you should do everything possible to expedite the purchase by (1) reassuring the customer that the purchase is the right one, (2) speeding delivery of the goods, and (3) overseeing any installation or implementation that may be required.

Provide Personal Service

In an age of "cookie-cutter" service that treats all customers the same, or that offers no service at all, providing personal service can be a powerful customer relations tool for winning customer loyalty. Everyone likes to be thought of as special or to get something "extra." You can meet these needs by addressing each customer by name, paying attention to individual preferences, and doing more than is expected.

Contrary to what you might think, providing a personal touch doesn't have to increase your costs. What it requires more than expenditures of money is thoughtfulness. Examples of this include:

- A restaurant owner remembering a customer's favorite table.
- A toy store that has the batteries a customer needs (especially on Christmas Eve) to go with the toys purchased.
- A pet-sitting service that also collects the client's mail and waters the plants while caring for the family pet.

- A computer store that includes "user-friendly" instructions with the computers it sells.

Since these "little things" often mean a lot to customers, paying attention to them can give you a distinct advantage over businesses that don't.

Answer Questions

Letting customers know that you're available to answer any questions that come up after the purchase is made is another way to serve your customers. Or you might want to set up a telephone/fax hot line that customers can use when they need to get information in a hurry. This not only provides customers with a sense of security, but can keep minor problems from becoming major ones. What's more, by keeping the lines of communication open, you stand a better chance of making more sales in the future.

Handle Complaints

In addition to answering questions, you must also be prepared to handle complaints. Complaints are a fact of business life. Even the most service-oriented businesses can expect to receive them. The issue isn't who's right or who's wrong, but what needs to be done to satisfy the customer. If there is something wrong with your products or services, you want to determine what you can do to improve them. If a customer is unhappy with a purchase, you must decide how you can remedy the situation.

To handle complaints more efficiently and to let your customers know that you're on their side, it helps to follow these guidelines:

1. Listen to what the customer is telling you without interruption.
2. Don't become defensive or angry.
3. Ask questions to get additional details, if necessary.
4. Show the customer that you care.
5. Take steps to resolve the problem as quickly as possible.
6. Thank the customer for bringing the problem to your attention.

Even if you think that the complaint is unjustified or that the customer is wasting your time, remember that there's something worse than having to deal with a dissatisfied customer who complains. That's having a dissatisfied customer who *doesn't* complain and just takes his or her business someplace else.

Solve Problems

The most successful sellers are problem solvers, not just when it comes to making the sale, but at helping customers put the products or services they've bought to best use. Instead of leaving customers to fend for themselves or saying, "That's your problem," they work with customers to find solutions to their problems. This joint approach to problem solving benefits not only the customer, but you as well. Customers who might not otherwise have come back buy again and recommend you to the people they know.

Stay in Touch

Instead of waiting for customers to contact you, take the initiative yourself. Staying in touch with customers on a regular basis shows that you care and puts you in a better position to anticipate customers' needs and to provide a high level of customer service.

Some of the ways that you can stay in touch include:

- Telephoning from time to time to see how customers are doing.
- Sending a card or a small gift at Christmas.
- Sending out mailings with up-to-date information on your products, services, and prices.
- Making periodic sales calls.

And, of course, whenever you make a new sale, it never hurts to send the customer a thank you note.

CUSTOMER SERVICE CHECKLIST

To determine if you're doing everything you can to build a positive relationship with each customer, answer the questions in the following Customer Service Checklist.

	Answer Yes or No
1. Is your selling strategy oriented toward satisfying each customers?	_____
2. Do you try to establish long-term relationships rather than just make a sale?	_____
3. During the selling process do you find out what the customer's needs are?	_____
4. Are you a good listener?	_____
5. Do you know how to interpret the verbal and nonverbal messages that customers send?	_____
6. Do you show customers the benefits of buying your products or services?	_____
7. Will you forgo making a sale if the purchase isn't right for the customer?	_____
8. After a sale is made, do you follow up on it later to see that the customer is pleased with the purchase?	_____
9. Do you provide personal service?	_____
10. Are you available to answer any questions that customers may have?	_____
11. Do you handle complaints quickly and courteously?	_____
12. Are you a problem solver?	_____
13. Do you make it a point to stay in touch with customers?	_____
14. Do you try to give customers something "extra" for their money?	_____
15. Do you genuinely care about your customers?	_____
16. Does your place of business convey a pleasing and professional image?	_____
17. Have you instructed your employees to treat all customers in a courteous and efficient manner?	_____
18. Do you believe that the customer is always right?	_____

15

Safeguarding Your Business

The very act of forming your own business entails risk. The rewards of prosperity and self-fulfillment must be balanced against the risks of financial loss and personal dissatisfaction. There are no sure things in business. Still, such factors as planning, experience, adequate financing, managerial expertise, creativity, and a willingness to work hard can swing the odds in your favor. For these to be effective, though, you need an ongoing program of risk management.

Suppose any of the following should happen:

- Your building is damaged by fire.
- A customer is hurt in you store.
- An employee steals merchandise.
- A car drives through your store window.
- Your accountant embezzles a large sum of money.
- An employee is injured on the job.
- Your store is burglarized.
- Your business is suffering because of shoplifting.
- A partner dies.

What would you do? A likely answer is, "Call my insurance

agent." But relying on insurance is only one of the ways to deal with these hazards.

RISK MANAGEMENT

An effective program of risk management enables you to cope with risks by eliminating them, reducing them, accepting them, or transferring them. These methods can be used singly or in combination, depending on the risk as well as on your own circumstances.

Eliminating the Risk

Certain risks can be entirely eliminated. Among these are the risk of employee injury because of substandard materials or unsafe equipment, the risk of customer injury because of a hazardous store layout, and the risk of fire because of faulty wiring. There's no excuse for allowing risks that are solely the result of negligence or indifference. One who persists in doing so could wind up not only financially liable but criminally liable as well. And it's not enough merely to carry insurance. Gross negligence, or the flagrant violation of health and safety standards, is sufficient ground for an insurance carrier to void your policy.

Reducing the Risks

It would be impossible for you to eliminate every business risk, even if you were aware of every one. Your best bet, then, is to reduce the risks. Close evaluation of your workplace, workers, and customers will enable you to take precautionary actions so as to reduce most of your business risks.

The risk of falling off a ladder can't be eliminated; but the use of safety ladders, with guard rails on either side, can reduce the risk. Keeping all merchandise boxes, cleaning supplies, tools, and electrical cords clear of customer walkways reduces the risk of having customers trip and injure themselves. The risks of breakage and theft can be reduced by displaying merchandise in locked cases. Electronic tags on merchandise, alert salespeople, closed-circuit cameras, burglar alarms, and security guards can also help you to combat theft.

Accepting the Risk

Self-insurance, a method whereby you create your own contingency fund to pay for whatever business losses might arise, is another way of coping with risk. This enables a business to protect itself while at the same time avoiding payment of insurance premiums. Unfortunately, the protection this method provides is usually inadequate. Given current high replacement costs for buildings, equipment, furniture, and fixtures, as well as the staggering amounts of some judgment claims in liability cases, a small business that relies solely on self-insurance could easily be wiped out.

A policy of accepting the risk might be applied, however, when the risk cannot be eliminated and buying outside insurance is not profitable. For instance, if your losses from shoplifting are less than the insurance premiums to protect yourself against it, accepting the losses makes more sense. Furthermore, even when you do carry insurance against a particular type of risk, part of the risk usually must be accepted because of the policy's deductible provision.

Transferring the Risk

The purchase of coverage from an insurance company enables businesses to transfer their risks. In exchange for a fee, the insurance company accepts the risks that the business wishes to be protected against. In effect, when you buy insurance you arrange to absorb small periodic losses (premiums) rather than a large uncertain loss. If your property is to be adequately protected and large damage claims that result from public liability or employee injury suits are to be avoided, insurance is a necessity.

TYPES OF INSURANCE COVERAGE

Fire Insurance

In a standard fire insurance policy your building, the property contained within it, and property temporarily removed from it because of fire are protected against damage inflicted by fire or lightning. This coverage does not extend to accounting records, bills, deeds, money, securities, or manuscripts. Nor are you protected against such hazards as windstorms, hail, smoke, explosions, vandalism, automatic sprinkler leakage, and malicious mischief. To guard excluded valuables and protect yourself against loss from these hazards, you must obtain additional coverage. Neither fire resulting from war nor actions taken under the orders of a civil authority are covered by insurance.

Depending on the terms of your policy, compensation may be made in any of three ways: (1) the insurance carrier may pay you the current cash value of the damaged property, (2) the property may be repaired or replaced, or (3) the property may be taken over by the insurer, who then reimburses you at its appraised value.

Most fire insurance policies are written for a three-year period, and both you and the insurer have the right to cancel. You may cancel your policy at any time. The insurer, however, must give you five days' notice before canceling. In either event, you will be reimbursed for any premiums that have been paid in advance. But if you are the one to cancel, a penalty as set forth in your policy may be assessed against your refund.

To keep your fire insurance policy valid, it's your responsibility to use all reasonable means to protect the insured property both before and after a fire. If you knowingly increase the fire hazard—by renting part of your building to a fireworks manufacturer, for example—this could void your policy. Hiding pertinent information from the insurer, or leaving your building unoccupied for more than 60 days, is also cause for voiding your policy.

Should it become necessary for you to file an insurance claim, you will be required to provide the insurance company with a complete inventory list, detailing the types, quantities, and values of the damaged property. Unless an extension is granted, you generally have 60 days in which to do this.

Liability Insurance

As the operator of your own business, you are responsible for the safety of your employees and customers. If a customer slips on a wet floor, you may be liable for damages. You're also responsible for the products or services you sell. For instance, the owner of a garage could be held liable for using a car wax that strips the paint off a customer's car, or if a mechanic forgets to set the hand brake on a car and it rolls into the street and causes an accident. In the first case, the garage owner might have to cover the cost of a new paint job. In the second, there's no telling how much the cost might be. Was the car damaged? Were other cars damaged? Was anyone injured in the accident? These are just the physical damages for which the garage owner may be liable. What about the mental anguish of the parties involved in the accident? By the time all the costs have been added in, the entire assets of the garage could be wiped out.

Most liability policies cover losses stemming from bodily injury or property damage claims, expenses for medical services required at the time of the accident, investigation, and court costs.

The actual amount that your policy will pay depends on both the limit per accident and the limit per person provided for in it. For example, if your policy has a per-accident limit of $1 million and a per-person limit of $300,000, and if one person receives a $500,000 judgment against you, the insurance company will pay only $300,000. This means you are responsible for paying the remaining $200,000 even though it is within your per-accident limit. The guide word here is *caution*. Make sure you understand and agree with any limitations in your policy. If the limit is $300,000 per person, is that adequate coverage?

If an accident does occur, even if it seems minor, contact your insurance agent immediately. This enables the insurance company to begin its investigation while the relevant information is readily available. Failure to notify the company can void your policy.

The most common types of liability insurance are:

- General liability insurance. The most far-reaching type of liability insurance available, it provides basic coverage against all liabilities not specifically excluded from the policy.

- Product liability insurance. This insurance protects you against financial loss in the event that someone is injured by a product you manufacture or distribute.

- Professional liability. For doctors, lawyers, consultants, and others who provide advice or information or perform a service, this insurance protects you against damage claims brought by dissatisfied clients.

Marine Insurance

To protect yourself against damage to your property while it is being transported from one place to another, you should obtain marine insurance. Originally issued to protect ship cargoes against the perils of the high seas, this type of insurance now covers property losses both on water and land. *Ocean marine insurance* protects property carried on board a ship at sea or in port. *Inland marine insurance* protects property being transported by ship, rail, truck, or plane.

Automobile Insurance

If you plan to use one or more cars or trucks in your business, automobile insurance is a must. Coverage can be provided to protect you against:

- Bodily injury claims.
- Property damage claims.
- Medical payments.
- Uninsured motorist damages.
- Damage to your vehicle.
- Towing costs.

The amount of coverage you need and the costs of an automobile insurance policy depend on:

- The number of cars or trucks being insured.
- Their value.
- The kinds of driving that will be done (making deliveries, hauling equipment, driving clients around).
- Your location.

When five or more motor vehicles are used in your business, you can generally insure them under a low-cost fleet policy. As far as deductibles go, the higher they are, the lower your premiums.

You may find that automobile insurance is a good buy even if you don't plan to use any motor vehicles in your business. This is because you could be held liable for employees or subcontractors who operate their own vehicles, or those of customers, while on company business.

Workers' Compensation Insurance

Common law requires that an employer (1) provide employees with a safe place to work, (2) hire competent co-workers, (3) provide safe tools, and (4) warn employees of existing danger. An employer who fails to do so is liable for damages, including claims for on-the-job injury and occupational diseases. Sometimes payment can be required for the remainder of the disabled worker's life.

Under workers' compensation insurance, the insurance pays all sums you are legally required to pay a claimant. One way to save money on this insurance is to make sure your employees are properly classified. Since rates vary with the degree of hazard associated with each occupational category, improperly classifying an employee in a high-risk occupation raises your rates. Another way to save money is to use safety measures that will lower your accident rate and thereby reduce premiums.

Business Interruption Insurance

Many business owners fail to purchase business interruption insurance because they don't think they need it. If a building burns down, they think a standard fire insurance policy will suffice. But what about the loss of business income during the months it takes to rebuild? What about the expenses that continue to mount up even though your doors are closed—taxes, interest on loans, salaries, rent, utilities? Yet not until it is too late does many a business owner realize that fire insurance alone isn't enough.

Only business interruption insurance covers your fixed expenses and expected profits during the time your business is closed down. And make sure that the policy is written to provide coverage in the event that your business isn't totally shut down, but is seriously disrupted. Some policies pay off only in the event of a total shutdown. You should also remember that an indirect peril could force you to suspend operations as well. What if an important supplier's or customer's plant burned down, temporarily interrupting your business? What if your power, water, or phone service were disrupted for a spell? Protection against these hazards can be written into your business interruption policy, but you have to ask for it.

Glass Insurance

Although it may seem insignificant, glass insurance is something most businesses should have. The costs of replacing broken plate glass windows, panels, doors, signs, and display cases are so high that you can't afford to be without it. Furthermore, delays in making the replacement can result in vandalism or theft, which in turn results in additional property loss.

A glass insurance policy covers the cost not only of replacing the glass itself, but of redoing any letter or ornamentation on the glass, installing the glass (including temporary glass or boards, if needed), and repairing any frame damage. The only exclusions in the standard all-risk glass insurance policy are for glass damage from fire or war. And, in the case of fire, your fire insurance policy provides coverage.

Fidelity Bonds

Most new business owners are unaware that, on the average, thefts by employees far surpass business losses from burglary, robbery, and shoplifting. The accountant who embezzles thousands of dollars and then goes to Acapulco and the salesclerk who dips into the cash drawer come readily to mind. Less obvious examples include:

- Putting fictitious employees on the payroll and pocketing their paychecks.
- Ringing up lower prices on merchandise sold to friends or accomplices.
- Stealing merchandise, equipment, or supplies.
- Misappropriating company property for personal use.
- Lying on expense vouchers.
- Falsifying time cards.

Unless you or members of your immediate family handle all phases of your business operation, you should obtain fidelity bond protection. This is available in three formats: individual bonds, schedule bonds, and blanket bonds. *Individual bonds* cover theft by a specific named individual. *Schedule bonds* list every name or position to be covered. *Blanket bonds*, the most encompassing of the three, cover all employes without reference to individual names or positions.

Before an employee is bonded, the insurance company issuing the bond conducts a character investigation to determine whether anything is known of past acts of dishonesty. Then, if the employee is deemed bondable, coverage is provided. If a prospective employee refuses to be bonded, this could be a tip-off that the applicant has something to hide.

Crime Insurance

Crime insurance covers you against business losses resulting from the criminal activities of people who aren't associated with your business. The three categories of crime insurance are burglary insurance, robbery insurance, and comprehensive insurance.

1. *Burglary insurance* protects your safes and inventory against thefts in which there is evidence of forcible entry. This means that, if a thief enters through an unlocked door or window without disturbing the premises, your burglary policy does not cover any losses. Nor does the standard burglary policy protect accounting records, manuscripts, or certain valuables, such as furs, that are kept in display windows. To cover these, additional insurance is necessary. Besides protecting you against losses from stolen property, burglary insurance provides coverage for damage sustained during the burglary.

2. *Robbery* differs from burglary in that it involves a face-to-face confrontation. The robber actually uses force, or the threat of violence, to take property from the person guarding it. A *robbery insurance* policy covers the money, property, or securities taken, as well as property damage that occurs during the robbery. Another feature of this policy is that it isn't limited to robberies that take place inside your building. Thus if you are robbed while making a delivery you are covered.

3. *Comprehensive insurance* is popular because, in addition to protecting you against burglary and robbery, it also protects against a variety of other hazards, including counterfeit money and forged checks. For instance, deception does not constitute robbery. If a con artist tricks you or an employee into parting with property, no force or threat of violence is involved. Therefore, it isn't a robbery, and unless you have a comprehensive policy you aren't covered. Coverage is also provided against the thief who gains entry to your business without any apparent use of force.

Personal Insurance

Just as there's a need to insure your property against loss, there's an equal need to insure both yourself and your employees. Group health and life insurance, a retirement plan, and key personnel insurance all help to do this. The need for these may seem a long way off, but more and more small businesses are offering an employee benefits package that includes health and life insurance as a way of retaining valued personnel. If you decide to incorporate a retirement plan too, there's another advantage. Contributions made to the plan for yourself and employees are deductible from your federal income tax.

Key personnel insurance, long a staple in the insurance portfolio of major corporations, can be just as necessary for the small business owner. Could your business survive the death or disability of a partner or a key employee? If not, key personnel insurance can at least ease the loss. The proceeds from the insurance are exempt from income tax and payable directly to the business. The policy itself has a cash value and may be used as loan collateral.

RECOGNIZING WARNING SIGNALS

The old adage that an ounce of prevention is worth a pound of cure readily pertains to risk management. But before you can take precautionary measures to head off an impending danger, you have to recognize the danger. The way to do this is to be alert to the warning signals around you. The following examples indicate a fire, accident, or theft waiting to happen—if it hasn't already:

Fire

1. Overloaded circuits.
2. Fuse blowouts.
3. Frayed electrical cords.
4. Overheating of equipment.
5. Fire extinguishers inoperative or inaccessible.
6. Trash piled up.
7. Smoking permitted in high-risk areas.
8. Improper procedures in use, storage, or disposal of flammable materials.
9. Power plant, heating, ventilation, and air conditioning equipment not checked at regular intervals.

Accident

1. Workers inadequately trained for their jobs.
2. Lack of safety rules or failure to enforce them.
3. Use of substandard materials or equipment.
4. Poor quality control.
5. A hazardous layout.
6. Admitting customers to the work area.
7. Letting customers use equipment themselves.
8. Lack of knowledge about products you sell.

Employee Theft

1. Inadequate employee reference checks.
2. An employee who refuses to take an annual vacation.
3. An employee who never leaves the work area during lunch.
4. An employee who always arrives at work early and stays late.
5. One employee handling all bookkeeping procedures.
6. Expenses that are higher than predicted.
7. Inventory shortages.
8. Finding merchandise or equipment in trash bins.
9. Checks and money orders left sitting on desktops.
10. Unfamiliar names on the payroll.
11. An increase in sales returns.
12. Slow collections.

On the surface, none of these examples is proof of embezzlement, but their occurrence does indicate the need for additional investigation or tightened management controls.

Crime

1. Accepting checks without asking to see proper identification.
2. Accepting checks that have been endorsed twice.
3. Accepting blank checks that don't have computer-coded characteristics.
4. Keeping large amounts of money in cash registers.
5. Inattention to customers when they:
   a. Wear loose clothing.
   b. Carry a large purse or open shopping bag.
   c. Seem nervous or anxious.
   d. Wander into a restricted area.
   e. Are left unsupervised in dressing rooms.
6. Easily removable tickets on merchandise.
7. Failure of the cash register operator to open and inspect items that might conceal stolen goods.
8. Messy displays that make it difficult to spot what's there and what's missing.
9. Employee unfamiliarity with the merchandise your store carries.

10. Poor lighting.
11. Unsuitable locks on doors and windows.
12. Loose handling of keys.

INSURANCE CHECKLIST

To make sure that you've adequately insured your business, use the following Insurance Checklist to indicate the coverage you need.

Type of Insurance	Purchase	Do Not Purchase
Property Insurance		
Fire	_____	_____
Windstorm	_____	_____
Hail	_____	_____
Smoke	_____	_____
Explosion	_____	_____
Vandalism	_____	_____
Water damage	_____	_____
Glass	_____	_____
Liability Insurance	_____	_____
Workers' Compensation	_____	_____
Business Interruption	_____	_____
Fidelity	_____	_____
Robbery	_____	_____
Burglary	_____	_____
Comprehensive	_____	_____
Personal		
Health	_____	_____
Life	_____	_____
Key personnel	_____	_____

16

Franchising

An alternative to forming your own business from scratch is to purchase a franchise. According to Department of Commerce statistics, franchising has grown to such proportions that franchised operations now account for annual sales totaling more than a third of all U.S. retail sales. Although commonly associated with fast food outlets, franchising's application is not limited to the food service industry. Franchises have become particularly visible in a variety of areas, including hotels and motels, print shops, automobile dealerships, service stations, beauty salons, travel agencies, convenience stores, employment agencies, accounting services, and real estate brokerages. In fact, there seem to be few, if indeed any, businesses that don't lend themselves to franchising. The most recent entrants have been the legal and medical professions.

The boom in franchising began shortly after World War II and has continued ever since, despite fluctuations in the economy and added government regulations. Franchising's boosters predict that the future will be even better since franchising offers investors job security and a hedge against inflation. Franchising's critics, on the other hand, are quick to point out that many who enter into franchising agreements end up working harder and earning less than they expected.

THE DEFINITION OF FRANCHISING

Franchising is a method of doing business whereby a company (the franchisor) grants to others (the franchisees) the rights to sell, distribute, or market the company's products or services. In so doing, franchisees are permitted to use the franchisor's name, trademarks, reputation, and selling techniques. To obtain these rights, each franchisee agrees to pay the franchisor a sum of money (the franchise fee), a percentage of annual gross sales, or both. Many franchisees agree to purchase equipment or supplies from the franchisor as well.

Franchisors view franchising as a way to expand their businesses without having to rely on loans or stock issues for the necessary capital. In addition to providing expansion capital, franchisees generally can be counted on to bring high levels of energy and commitment to the company—a real plus, particularly if the going gets rough. Franchisees, for their part, view franchising as a way to tap into a good thing—a sort of hitch-your-wagon-to-a-going-concern-strategy.

THE PRICE

How much does it cost to purchase a franchise? That depends. Your initial investment can vary from a few thousand dollars to upward of a million. On top of that is the annual percentage of gross sales, or royalty fee, required by most franchisors. This can be as high as 18 percent. Other charges may also be stipulated in the franchise agreement. Franchising, albeit an alternative to forming your own business from scratch, is not necessarily a cheap alternative.

FRANCHISING'S ADVANTAGES AND DISADVANTAGES

To determine whether the franchising route is right for you, take a look at both the advantages and disadvantages of buying a franchise.

The Advantages

Only limited experience is needed. As a franchisee you have access to the franchisor's experience. Instead of spending years learning the ropes in your intended business, you can be running it.

Training and continued assistance are provided. Rather than being left to sink or swim on your own, you have the franchisor there to provide additional support. This includes training programs and the ongoing services of consultants.

Financing is often available. The franchisor may permit you to make partial payment of your start-up costs (construction, equipment, inventory, promotion, and so on) and defer the balance over a period of years. This reduces the amount of capital immediately needed for your initial investment.

Purchasing power can be increased. It's often possible to purchase the products, supplies, equipment, and services used in your business directly from the franchisor at reduced rates. This enables you to stretch your dollars farther.

Promotion is generally strong. Franchisors put a great deal of effort into making their companies' names recognizable to the public. As a result of the franchisor's promotional campaign, your business benefits.

Customer acceptance is high. Since the goods and services of the franchisor are proven and well known, your business has virtually instant pulling power. Whereas a new business might spend years developing its reputation, yours is already established.

The Disadvantages

Guidelines must be followed. The franchisor sets the rules; your freedom to make decisions is limited by the necessity to follow standardized procedures and offer specific products or services.

Contracts tend to favor the franchisor. Since the franchise agreement is prepared by the franchisor, your bargaining power may be less than equal. Should a dispute arise, the franchisor generally has the edge.

Profits are shared with the franchisor. Normally franchisees are required to pay the franchisor a percentage of annual gross sales, thus reducing their own profits. In the event that your business fails to make a profit, this percentage must still be paid.

Transfer of ownership is limited. Your right to dispose of your franchise is restricted by the provisions of the franchise agreement. This means you may not be permitted to sell it to the highest bidder, bequeath it to a relative or friend in your will, or even give it away without the franchisor's approval.

Purchasing power can be reduced. Some franchisees have been required to purchase the products, supplies, equipment, and services used in their businesses only from the franchisor, even when other sources could provide them for less. The courts now consider such tie-in practices to be illegal, and you should be wary of any agreement that imposes them.

Other franchisees' actions reflect on you. A consumer who receives poor service in another one of the franchisor's outlets is likely to assume your franchise offers poor service too. Your business suffers as a result, regardless of its merits.

Paperwork is time-consuming. The franchisor requires that you fill out a variety of reports, which takes time. Unless you're organized, you could end up buried under an avalanche of paperwork.

THE FRANCHISE AGREEMENT

The franchise agreement forms the basis for your relationship with the franchisor. Therefore, it must state clearly and in adequate detail the rights and responsibilities of both parties to the agreement. Anything that's ambiguous should be clarified at the outset. Waiting until later to straighten it out can have unfortunate consequences. Make sure that you are willing to accept *all* of the provisions contained in the contract. Once you've signed the agreement, you will be bound by it. If you find a clause unreasonable, try to have it deleted from the contract or modified. Barring these possibilities, you may decide not to enter into an agreement with the franchisor. The best way to protect yourself is to obtain the advice of an attorney before signing any papers.

In evaluating the merits of a particular franchise agreement, you should give careful attention to the following provisions in the agreement:

Total franchise cost. How much money does it really take to own and operate the franchise? Not just for the franchise fee, but for everything. It's surprising how many people fail to take into consideration all the charges that may be assessed. Among these are:

- Franchise fee, granting you the right to engage in business as a franchised operation.
- Physical facilities fees, covering the costs of establishing you in an appropriate location (marketing research, construction, lease, and so on).

- **Equipment and fixtures cost,** covering the costs of outfitting your building.

- **Inventory and supplies cost,** covering the costs of stocking your business with the necessary inventory and supplies.

- **Royalty payments,** representing a percentage of annual gross sales (one of the requirements for operating the franchise).

- **Promotion costs,** covering your share of the advertising costs. (These may be included in the royalty payments.)

- **Finance charges,** including all interest due on loans made to the franchisee.

Only when you have added up all these charges (and any others that may be levied) can you determine the total franchise cost.

Contract life.   What is the life of the contract? Does your right to operate the franchise extend indefinitely, or is it limited to a specific number of years? What are the renewal provisions? The average contract life, excluding renewal provisions, is 15 years.

Termination clause.   Often referred to as the "franchisor's exit clause," the termination clause should be gone over with great care. Essentially, what it represents is the franchisor's right to terminate your relationship by canceling your contract or failing to renew it. This right is retained by the franchisor on the grounds that it is the only way to maintain standards and protect the company's image. Unfortunately, it can also be used to punish franchisees who allegedly fall out of line, even though there may be no good cause for doing so.

For your protection make note of these four points:

1. The actions on your part that constitute grounds for termination by the franchisor.

2. The method that will be used to determine the value of the franchise in the event of termination (original cost or fair market value).

3. Whether you have the right to terminate the agreement yourself and at what cost.

4. Whether you have the right, upon termination, to enter into direct competition with the franchisor in the franchise area.

Transfer of ownership.   Do you have the right to sell or otherwise transfer ownership of the franchise to another party? In the majority of agreements, the franchisor reserves the right to buy back the franchise when the contract is terminated—often at the original price. Thus after investing several years' worth of time and money into your franchise, you could end up getting back only what you paid for it.

Franchise territory. The franchise territory is the selling area in which you are licensed to operate your franchise. In evaluating a prospective territory, you should determine the following:

1. Its sales potential (given local consumer demand and competition).
2. The characteristics (demographics and psychographics) of the neighborhood.
3. The territory's projected market growth.
4. Whether the franchisor is licensing others in the same territory.
5. Your right to open additional franchises in your territory or in other territories. Under existing antitrust laws, the franchisor has almost no legal power to stop you from branching out into other areas. However, bucking the franchise system is sure to strain your relationship.

Procedures. The procedures by which your franchise is expected to operate are included in the franchise agreement and/or the company's procedures manual. These can cover anything from the way to greet a customer to the way to keep the books. To safeguard your sanity later, take the time to familiarize yourself with them before you purchase the franchise. Remember that your way of doing business has to be compatible with the franchisor's way of doing business; otherwise, you're in for trouble.

Management training and assistance. What kind of management training and support can you count on the franchisor to provide? Some training programs are quite extensive, including one or more weeks at the franchisor's training headquarters, on-the-job training in an established franchise outlet, and continuing guidance once you're set up in your own franchise. Other training programs consist of little more than a few stapled-together pages of information, bolstered by an imaginary support system. Make sure the full details of the franchisor's training and assistance programs are spelled out in advance—and included in your contract. And don't forget to find out who foots the bill for the costs.

Promotional activities. What activities is the franchisor engaging in to promote the company's name and develop goodwill? Is advertising primarily at the local and regional level, or does it extend nationwide and beyond? Since one of the major selling points of a franchise is that it has a recognizable name, backed up by solid promotion, you need to know in advance the nature and extent of the company's promotional activities. And, once again, the matter of who pays for them comes up. Is your contribution included in the royalty fee, or is it an additional percentage of gross sales on top of that?

The franchise agreement merely sets down on paper the terms and conditions of the franchise relationship. As such, it isn't to be regarded with awe, but is to be explored as fully as possible. Don't let a lot of pages or legal jargon keep you from gaining a complete understanding of the agreement's contents. The best way to avoid getting burned is to enter into the relationship with your eyes open.

HOW TO FIND FRANCHISE OPPORTUNITIES

You can refer to numerous sources of information for help in finding franchise opportunities. The major sources are:

- Newspapers.
- Franchisors.
- Trade publications.
- Franchise associations.
- Franchise specialists.
- Your banker.
- The government.

Newspapers.   Chances are that you've already seen a variety of franchise offerings listed in the financial or classified section of your local newspaper.

Franchisors.   If you already have a particular industry in mind, write directly to the franchisors in that field for details about the requirements for obtaining a franchise. By writing to more than one company, you can compare opportunities.

Trade publications.   Read the trade publications for the industries that appeal to you. Franchisors seeking to expand their businesses will normally advertise in these.

Franchise associations.   Franchise associations publish magazines and reports on franchising and sponsor exhibitions where you can meet with franchisor representatives.

Franchise specialists. For a fee, specialists in the area of franchising will help you find and research franchise opportunities. Their services include obtaining financial and marketing data on the companies being considered and providing recommendations.

Your banker. Your banker is tuned into the business community and probably can provide you with information on current franchise offerings or the names of people to contact.

The government. Government sources ranging from the Postal Service to the Federal Trade Commission can provide you with information on franchising. Probably the best one to start with is the Small Business Administration.

FRANCHISING CHECKLIST

Evaluating a franchise requires a clear head. Keeping track of all the information, weighing the pros and cons, and listening to your own feelings isn't easy. The Franchising Checklist should help you bring order out of the chaos.

	Answer Yes or No
1. Has the franchisor been in business long enough to have established a good reputation?	_____
2. Have you checked the Better Business Bureau, the Chamber of Commerce, Dun & Bradstreet, or your banker to find out about the franchisor's business reputation and credit rating?	_____
3. Has the franchisor shown you certified figures on the net profits of one or more going operations? Have you checked them yourself?	_____
4. Has the franchisor given you a specimen contract to study with the advice of counsel?	_____
5. Has the product or service been on the market long enough to gain good consumer acceptance?	_____
6. Would you buy the product or service on its merits?	_____
7. Is the product or service protected by a patent?	_____
8. Does product liability insurance protect both you and the franchisor?	_____

	Answer Yes or No

9. Does the contract give you an exclusive territory for the life of the franchise? _____

10. Does the territory provide adequate sales potential? _____

11. Have you made any study to determine whether the product or service you propose to sell has a market in your territory at the price you will have to charge? _____

12. Will you be compelled to sell any new products or services introduced by the franchisor after you have opened the business? _____

13. If there is an annual sales quota, can you retain your franchise if it is not met? _____

14. Does the franchise fee seem reasonable? _____

15. Do continuing royalties or payments of percentages of gross sales appear reasonable? _____

16. Does the cash investment include payment for fixtures and equipment? _____

17. Can you purchase supplies from another source when available at a lower price? _____

18. If you will be required to participate in company promotion and publicity by contributing to an advertising fund, will you have the right to veto any increase to the fund? _____

19. Will your training include an opportunity to observe and work with a successful franchise for a time? _____

20. Does the franchisor provide continuing assistance through supervisors who visit regularly? _____

21. Is the franchise agreement renewable? _____

22. Can you terminate the agreement if for some reason you are not happy about it? _____

23. May you sell the business to anyone you please? _____

24. Does your attorney approve of the contract? _____

17

Getting Help

The major cause of most business failures is management that lacks the knowledge, skills, experience, or simply the time needed to run a business efficiently. Since new businesses can rarely afford to hire the specialists who enable big business to carry out its objectives, they are at a distinct disadvantage. However, the way to compensate for this, and still keep payroll expenses to a minimum, is to utilize outside services.

Many outside services are willing and eager to help your business succeed. Whether you need help in obtaining financing, keeping your books in order, coming up with new concepts for products and ways to promote your business, training and motivating personnel, or solving a variety of business problems, there are services available. Some of these services cost money, but surprisingly many of them are provided free of charge.

SOURCES OF OUTSIDE HELP

Here are some of the individuals and institutions that can assist you in operating your business, listed in alphabetical order:

- Accountants.
- Advertising agencies.
- Attorneys.
- Bankers.
- Chambers of commerce.

- Colleges and universities.
- Government agencies, including the Department of Commerce, economic development offices, Federal Trade Commission, Government Printing Office, Internal Revenue Service, International Trade Administration, Small Business Administration, and Small Business Development Centers.
- Insurance agents.
- Libraries.
- Management and marketing consultants.
- Temporary help services.
- Trade associations.

Each source can provide you with specific and useful information that otherwise might not be readily accessible to your business.

ACCOUNTANTS

An accountant can be instrumental in helping you to keep your business operating on a sound financial basis. Even if you are already familiar with recordkeeping procedures, or employ a bookkeeper to maintain your records, the services of an outside accountant may still be required. In addition to designing an accounting system that's suitable for your specific needs, an accountant can also assist in the following areas:

- Determining cash requirements.
- Budgeting.
- Forecasting.
- Controlling costs.
- Preparing financial statements.
- Interpreting financial data.
- Obtaining loans.
- Preparing tax returns.

How to Locate

You can find public accountants listed in the *Yellow Pages* of the telephone directory, but for best results it's advisable to try to locate one through a personal recommendation. Ask your banker or attorney to suggest an accountant. Since their work causes them to communicate with accountants regularly, both should be able to provide the names of accountants who can meet your requirements. Another approach is to contact one of the national or state accounting associations. One of the larger associations is:

American Institute of Certified Public Accountants
1211 Avenue of the Americas
New York, NY 10036

ADVERTISING AGENCIES

An advertising agency can help you to plan, produce, and place your business's advertising. Advertising agencies perform the following activities:

- Develop promotional strategies.
- Create advertising pieces (writing copy, designing graphics and layout, producing the finished product).
- Choose the appropriate media.
- Make sure that ads are run according to schedule.

Whether you need to use an advertising agency depends on the amount of advertising you intend to do.

How to Locate

To find out which advertising agencies offer which services and how to contact them, check the *Standard Directory of Advertising Agencies*, available at many public libraries. Another source of agency information is to talk to media sales representatives and get their opinions about the various advertising agencies. The advertising agencies in your area should also be listed in the *Yellow Pages*.

ATTORNEYS

An attorney can be useful to your business from the very start, helping you to determine which legal form of business is right for you, drawing up agreements, filing government paperwork, negotiating the lease or purchase of your building. Later on your attorney can continue to help by:

- Representing you in court.
- Providing legal advice.
- Interpreting legal documents.
- Assisting in tax planning.
- Helping you to comply with employment laws.
- Working out arrangements with creditors.
- Reorganizing the business, if needed.

How to Locate

Your accountant or banker should be able to recommend an attorney. If not, your state's bar association can provide you with the names of attorneys in your area. Other sources of information include business acquaintances, friends, and the *Yellow Pages*.

BANKERS

Your banker can be a valuable ally to your business, if you take the time to establish good rapport—preferably before you ask for a loan. The advice or information your banker can provide includes:

- How to open a checking account.
- How to obtain a line of credit.
- How to apply for a loan.
- How to prepare financial reports.
- How to bill customers.
- How to set up your payroll.

Furthermore, since bankers are constantly interacting with various segments of the community, your banker is likely to hear news that affects your business before you do.

CHAMBERS OF COMMERCE

Chambers of commerce are traditionally the information agencies of a community. Each chamber's goal is to represent and promote its area's economy, to encourage business and industrial investment, and to provide employment. As a new business owner, you should get in touch with your local chamber to find out what it has to offer (moral support, research data, general information about the community, or whatever). You might also decide to become a member. Chambers of commerce offer these benefits:

- They promote local businesses.
- They protect business interests.
- They act as the political voice of the business community.
- They are businesses united together.

COLLEGES AND UNIVERSITIES

The colleges and universities in your area are a vast resource of information, skills, and training. They offer access to:

- The school's library for books, periodicals, government reports, reference works, maps, charts, audiovisual aids.
- Professional consultants in a variety of business-related areas.
- Labor in the form of students who are receiving training in your field.
- Additional education in the form of classes in management theory, business operations, advertising, and so on.
- Seminars especially for small business owners (often tied to the Small Business Administration).

GOVERNMENT AGENCIES

Agencies of government at the local, state, and federal levels can provide you with an abundance of useful information at little or no cost.

Department of Commerce

One government agency that specializes in businesses' concerns, the Department of Commerce oversees the research and distribution of information of direct interest to the economic community. This data is collected and made available to the public in the form of publications and reports, including:

- *Survey of Current Business,* a monthly periodical that provides updates on changes in the nation's economy and the levels of business production and distribution.

- *Census Bureau Reports,* covering such areas as population statistics (age, income, level of education, family status, and other demographic data) and manufacturing, business, and agricultural trends.

In addition to these reports, Commerce Department specialists can advise you in such specific areas as domestic and foreign market opportunities, contacting foreign representatives, and deciphering tariff and trade regulations.

How to Locate

Department of Commerce publications are available at many public libraries or at the various department offices located throughout the United States. To find out the office that's closest to you, check your local phone directory white pages under "United States Government" or write to the Department of Commerce in Washington, D.C.

Economic Development Offices

Many communities maintain their own economic development offices. These differ from chambers of commerce in that they are maintained by local governments rather than local businesses. They can provide you with current statistical information regarding the economy, building activity, housing units, sales trends, population demographics, zoning, transportation, utilities, labor force, wages and salaries, community services, banks and savings and loan associations, traffic flows, and important telephone numbers.

Federal Trade Commission

The Federal Trade Commission regulates trade practices to protect the public against unfair methods of competition. It is empowered to collect information pertaining to business conduct and activities and distribute this to both government and the public. The information that is available includes guidelines on what constitutes deceptive pricing, deceptive guarantees, bait advertising, and other illegal practices. For more information, write to: The Federal Trade Commission, Washington, D.C. 20580.

Government Printing Office

The Government Printing Office oversees the publication and distribution of government documents, pamphlets, reports, and books on a variety of subjects, many of which are directly related to business. These are for sale, usually at nominal prices, at local Government Printing Office bookstores, which are generally located in federal buildings. If one isn't near you, or it doesn't stock a publication you want, write directly to the U.S. Government Printing Office, Superintendent of Documents, Washington, D.C. 20402. You will be sent a catalog of the publications available and any publications that you request.

Internal Revenue Service

The Internal Revenue Service can answer any questions you have concerning your federal income taxes. Tax specialists in local IRS offices can handle specific questions, or you can refer to any of the numerous IRS guides and publications. One particularly valuable guide is the *Tax Guide for Small Businesses*, which is updated annually. It contains approximately 200 pages of information covering such subjects as books and records, accounting periods, determining gross profit, deductible expenses, depreciation, tax credits, and ways to report income. This is available free of charge at your local IRS office. Some of the other IRS publications are listed at the end of this chapter.

International Trade Administration

The International Trade Administration, operating under the auspices of the Department of Commerce, can provide you with a wealth of information concerning trade and investment opportunities abroad, foreign markets, financing for exporters, export documentation and licensing requirements, and so on. ITA district offices are located throughout the United States and Puerto Rico.

In addition to its counseling services and publications, the ITA also has Country Desk Officers headquartered in Washington, D.C., who track world economic trends. Desk officers maintain up-to-date information on the commercial conditions in their assigned countries and can provide you with the data you need about countries in which you are planning to sell your goods or services.

For more information on the ITA or its Country Desk organization, contact the Department of Commerce.

Small Business Administration

The Small Business Administration is designed to aid small businesses in the following ways:

- Helping to obtain financing.
- Providing management and technical assistance.
- Conducting business seminars and workshops.
- Assisting in procuring government contracts.

This is achieved through the operation of more than 100 district offices, the distribution of publications, and the activities of the Service Corps of Retired Executives (SCORE) and the Active Corps of Executives (ACE), volunteer groups of professionals who assist the SBA in advising small businesses.

Financing by the SBA takes the form of direct and indirect loans to businesses. Loan proceeds can be used for working capital, for purchase of inventory, equipment, and supplies, or for building construction or expansion. The SBA also makes loans to help small businesses comply with federal air and water pollution regulations and meet occupational health and safety standards. In addition, economic opportunity loans are available to help persons who are socially or economically disadvantaged. Although money for venture or high-risk investments is difficult to obtain from the SBA, it licenses Small Business Investment Companies (SBICs), which *do* make such loans. For more information about SBA or SBIC lending practices, check Chapter 8.

The SBA offers *management and technical assistance* in many forms. There are numerous titles to choose from in its list of business publications. SBA form 115A lists publications that are for sale for a nominal fee. A sampling of the titles is shown at the end of this chapter.

In-depth counseling is also provided by SBA management assistance staff, augmented by SCORE and ACE volunteers. Among the subject areas in which you can receive guidance are opening a business, marketing, advertising, profit goals, borrowing, accounting, bookkeeping, personnel, inventory controls, customer analysis, forecasting, and insurance. Meetings with these business counselors can be arranged through your local SBA field office. There is no charge for their services.

To help small entrepreneurs protect their investments, the SBA offers a variety of *seminars and workshops*. One that is of particular interest to prospective business owners is the Pre-Business Workshop. This is a free one-day session in which participants are helped to determine their readiness to go into business and advised of the steps involved in getting started. Once the decision is made to go ahead, the SBA assists participants in developing workable business plans. Other topics covered in workshops or seminars include:

- Sales Promotion and Advertising.
- Basic Business Operations.
- Business Planning.
- Women in Business.
- Foreign Trade.
- Retail Store Security.

The SBA's procurement assistance officers can guide you in the process of selling to the government and obtaining *government contracts*. They can help you to win subcontracting assignments too. The SBA works closely with large government contractors to make sure that they use qualified small businesses as subcontractors on their projects.

Small Business Development Centers

Entrepreneurs seeking one-on-one business consulting services, technical assistance, and training can find this and more at small business development centers (SBDCs) throughout the United States. Generally operated by colleges and universities, SBDCs draw on a combination of government, education, and private sector resources to provide business owners with such services as:

- Individualized counseling.
- Assistance in planning.
- Workshops and seminars.
- On-site employee training.
- Information about government programs.
- Referrals and networking opportunities.
- Access to economic and business data—books, reports, pamphlets, software, video, and cassette programs.

The goal of the small business development centers is to stimulate the economy by helping small and medium-sized businesses to function more effectively. Toward this end, SBDC counselors and outside experts in such areas as accounting, law, computers, marketing, and finance work closely with entrepreneurs to achieve their goals. Serving the needs of both prospective and current entrepreneurs, SBDCs assist small businesses at all stages of their development.

To find out if there's an SBDC near you, check the list at the end of this chapter or contact your local college's business department for information.

INSURANCE AGENTS

An insurance agent can analyze your business's specific needs and help you to obtain adequate coverage. Aspects of risk management that you should discuss with your agent include how to protect your assets, workers, and earnings and how to stay in compliance with the law. Since the welfare of your business is dependent on the safeguards you provide, finding a good insurance agent should be given a high priority.

How to Locate

The best ways to find an insurance agent are though personal recommendations (your accountant, attorney, or banker may be able to suggest someone) and comparison shopping. Talking to different agents not only lets you evaluate the levels of coverage and compare the costs of different insurance plans but gives you an idea of which agent is the most knowledgeable about your type of business. You can find the names of insurance agents and companies in the *Yellow Pages*.

LIBRARIES

Much of the information you need in order to operate your business can be obtained free of charge from libraries. The answers to many of your everyday business questions can be found not only in the books but in the assortment of magazines, newspapers, reference works, government publications, maps, charts, and audio/visual aids that are available. Management and marketing approaches, technical explanations, statistical data, industry information, trends and economic forecasts are just some of the subject areas in which you can find information.

How to Locate

In addition to public libraries, there are also libraries sponsored by colleges and universities, private industry, trade and professional associations, labor unions, and research centers. The most useful of these generally have separate business reference sections. To find the libraries in your area, check your local telephone directory.

MANAGEMENT AND MARKETING CONSULTANTS

Management and marketing consultants can detect weaknesses in your methods of operation or your marketing strategy and recommend corrective measures. They can also be of help *before* problems arise, providing advice on new product development, marketing research, business expansion, administration, employee motivation, cost control, security, and so on.

Many businesses make a practice of calling in a management or marketing consultant whenever a major decision in these areas needs to be made. This enables the business owner to benefit not only from the consultant's knowledge and experience, but from something equally valuable: the consultant's objectivity. Unlike employees, consultants have nothing to gain or lose from the outcome of a decision. Furthermore, the variety of their contacts in the business community usually gives them a broader perspective.

How to Locate

The best way to locate a management or marketing consultant is through recommendations, preferably from the consultant's satisfied clients. Otherwise, you can check the listings in one of the several directories of consultants available at public libraries or in the *Yellow Pages.*

TEMPORARY HELP SERVICES

There are temporary help service firms throughout the United States, providing experienced and well-qualified temporary help in a moment's notice. You may contract for a typist, receptionist, bookkeeper, salesperson, engineer, machinist, or other office, professional, and industrial workers. The temporary help service firm takes care of all screening, interviewing, and testing of applicants, as well as the checking of references.

How to Locate

Temporary help service firms can be located through personal recommendations, local chambers of commerce, or the *Yellow Pages*.

TRADE ASSOCIATIONS

Trade associations are organizations whose members are in the same business or industry (garment industry, banking and finance, restaurants, automotive repair). The concerns and services of trade associations are directed at helping members to improve their operating efficiency and cope with business problems. This help is in the form of:

- Accounting services. Providing accounting forms and manuals, ratio data, cost studies, and consultations.
- Advertising and marketing services. Providing advertising materials and forecasts of future demand levels and trends.
- Publicity and public relations activities. Providing members and the mass media with information about industry activities.
- Educational programs. Providing a variety of training courses and aids to assist business owners and employees in developing their skills.
- Research activities. Providing members and government with statistics about the industry—method of operation, product standards, certifying and grading, and so on.
- Employee relations programs. Providing members with information about industry wages, work schedules, and fringe benefits as well as assisting in the negotiation of labor contracts.
- Government relations programs. Providing members with a collective voice to use in communicating with the government and informing members of government actions pertaining to their businesses.

In addition, trade associations are active in public service, consumerism, and environmental safety. Of course, not all associations provide all these services. To find out which ones are provided, contact the association in your field of business.

How to Locate

To obtain information on trade associations or find out which ones represent your industry, check these publications available at most public libraries:

- *National Trade and Professional Associations of the United States and Canada*, Columbia Books, Inc., Publishers, Washington, D.C.
- *Encyclopedia of Associations*, Gale Research Inc., Detroit, Mich.

PUBLICATIONS

The following is a sampling of IRS and SBA publications, as well as lists of SBA field offices and SBDC lead centers.

IRS Tax Publications

The following publications can provide you with additional information about business taxation. These publications should be available at your local IRS office; if not, you can obtain them by writing to the Internal Revenue Service, Washington, D.C. 20224.

Title	No.
Your Rights as a Taxpayer	1
Employer's Tax Guide (Circular E)	15
Your Federal Income Tax	17
Tax Guide for Small Business	334
Fuel Tax Credits and Refunds	378
Travel, Entertainment and Gift Expenses	463
Tax Withholding and Estimated Tax	505
Excise Taxes	510
Moving Expenses	521
Tax Information on Selling Your Home	523
Taxable and Nontaxable Income	525
Charitable Contributions	526
Residential Rental Property	527
Miscellaneous Deductions	529
Tax Information for Homeowners	530
Self-Employment Tax	533
Depreciation	534
Business Expenses	535
Net Operating Losses	536
Accounting Periods and Methods	538

Title	No.
Tax Information on Partnerships	541
Tax Information on Corporations	542
Sales and Other Dispositions of Assets	544
Nonbusiness Disasters, Casualties, and Thefts	547
Investment Income and Expenses	550
Basis of Assets	551
Recordkeeping for Individuals	552
Federal Tax Information on Community Property	555
Examinations of Returns, Appeal Rights, and Claims for Refund	556
Retirement Plans for the Self-Employed	560
Taxpayers Starting a Business	583
The Collection Process (Income Tax Accounts)	586A
Business Use of Your Home	587
Tax Information on S Corporations	589
Individual Retirement Arrangements (IRAs)	590
The Collection Process (Employment Tax Accounts)	594
Guide to Free Tax Services	910
Tax Information for Direct Sellers	911
Business Use of a Car	917
Employment Taxes for Household Employers	926
Business Reporting	937
How to Begin Depreciating Your Property	946
Filing Requirements for Employee Benefit Plans	1048
Per Diem Rates	1542

Small Business Administration Publications

The following publications can provide you with additional information about small business operations. To purchase these nominally priced publications, write to the Small Business Administration, Washington D.C. 20417 to obtain an order form.

Title	No.
Products/Ideas/Inventions	
Ideas into Dollars	PI1
Avoiding Patent, Trademark and Copyright Problems	PI2
Trademarks and Business Goodwill	PI3
Financial Management	
ABC's of Borrowing	FM1
Profit Costing and Pricing for Manufacturers	FM2
Basic Budgets for Profit Planning	FM3
Understanding Cash Flow	FM4

Title	No.
A Venture Capital Primer for Small Business	FM5
Accounting Services for Small Service Firms	FM6
Analyze Your Records to Reduce Costs	FM7
Budgeting in a Small Service Firm	FM8
Sound Cash Management and Borrowing	FM9
Record Keeping in a Small Business	FM10
Simple Break-Even Analysis for Small Stores	FM11
A Pricing Checklist for Small Retailers	FM12
Pricing Your Products and Services Profitably	FM13

Management and Planning

Effective Business Communications	MP1
Locating or Relocating Your Business	MP2
Problems in Managing a Family-Owned Business	MP3
Business Plan for Small Manufacturers	MP4
Business Plan for Small Construction Firms	MP5
Planning and Goal Setting for Small Business	MP6
Should You Lease or Buy Equipment?	MP8
Business Plan for Retailers	MP9
Choosing a Retail Location	MP10
Business Plan for Small Service Firms	MP11
Checklist for Going into Business	MP12
How to Get Started with a Small Business Computer	MP14
The Business Plan for Home-Based Business	MP15
How to Buy or Sell a Business	MP16
Purchasing for Owners of Small Plants	MP17
Buying for Retail stores	MP18
Small Business Decision Making	MP19
Business Continuation Planning	MP20
Developing a Strategic Business Plan	MP21
Inventory Management	MP22
Techniques for Problem Solving	MP23
Techniques for Productivity Improvement	MP24
Selecting the Legal Structure for Your Business	MP25
Evaluating Franchise Opportunities	MP26
Small Business Risk Management Guide	MP28
Quality Child Care Makes Good Business Sense	MP29

Marketing

Creative Selling: The Competitive Edge	MT1
Marketing for Small Business: An Overview	MT2
Is the Independent Sales Agent for You?	MT3
Marketing Checklist for Small Retailers	MT4
Researching Your Market	MT8
Selling by Mail Order	MT9
Market Overseas with U.S. Government Help	MT10

Title	No.
Advertising	MT11
Crime Prevention	
Curtailing Crime—Inside and Out	CP2
A Small Business Guide to Computer Security	CP3
Personnel Management	
Checklist for Developing a Training Program	PM1
Employees: How to Find and Pay Them	PM2
Managing Employee Benefits	PM3

SBA FIELD OFFICES

Regional Offices

Region I
155 Federal Street
9th Floor
Boston, MA 02110
617/451-2030

Region II
26 Federal Plaza Room 31-08
New York, NY 10278
212/264-7772

Region III
Allendale Square
Suite 201
475 Allendale Road
King of Prussia, PA 19406
215/962-3805

Region IV
1375 Peachtree Street, NE
5th Floor
Atlanta, GA 30367-8102
404/347-2797

Region V
300 S. Riverside Plaza
Suite 1975
Chicago, IL 60606-6611
312/353-0359

Region VI
8625 King George Dr.
Building C
Dallas, TX 75235-3391
214/767-7643

Region VII
911 Walnut Street
13th Floor
Kansas City, MO 64106
816/426-2989

Region VIII
999 18th Street
Suite 701, N. Tower
Denver, CO 80202
303/294-7001

Region IX
71 Stevenson Street
San Francisco, CA 94105-2939
415/744-6402

Region X
2615 Fourth Avenue
Room 440
Seattle, WA 98121
206/442-5676

Disaster Area Offices

Area 1: Regions I-II
360 Rainbow Boulevard S.
3rd Floor
Niagara Falls, NY 14303
716/282-4612
In NY: 1-800-221-2091
Outside NY: 1-800-221-2093

Area 2: Regions III-V
One Baltimore Place
Suite 300
Atlanta, GA 30308
404/347-3771

Area 3: Regions VI-VII
4400 Amon Carter Boulevard
Suite 102
Ft. Worth, TX 76155
817/267-1888

Area 4: Regions VIII-X
1825 Bell Street
Suite 208
P.O. Box 13795
Sacramento, CA 95825
916/978-4578

District, Branch, and Post-of-Duty Offices

Alabama
2121 8th Avenue North
Suite 200
Birmingham, AL 35203-2398
205/731-1344

Alaska
222 W. 8th Avenue
Room A36
Anchorage, AK 99501
907/271-4022

Arizona
2005 N. Central Avenue
5th Floor
Phoenix, AZ 85004
602/379-3737

300 W. Congress Street
Room 3V
Tucson, AZ 85701-1319
602/670-6715

Arkansas
320 W. Capital Avenue
Room 601
Little Rock, AR 72201
501/378-5277

California
211 Main Street
4th Floor
San Francisco, CA 94105-1988
415/744-6801

2719 N. Air Fresno Drive
Suite 107
Fresno, CA 93727-1547
209/487-5189

660 J Street
Room 215
Sacramento, CA 95814
916/551-1426

880 Front Street
Suite 4-S-29
San Diego, CA 92188
619/557-5440

330 N. Brand Boulevard
Glendale, CA 91203
213/894-2956

901 W. Civic Center Drive
Suite 160
Santa Ana, CA 92703
714/836-2494

Colorado
721 19th Street
Room 407
Denver, CO 80201-0660
303/844-2607

Connecticut
330 Main Street
2nd Floor
Hartford, CT 06106
203/240-4700

Delaware
920 N. King Street
Room 412
Wilmington, DE 19801
302/573-6294

District of Columbia
1111 18th Street, NW
Sixth Floor
Washington, DC 20036
202/634-1500

Florida
7825 Baymeadows Way
Suite 100-B
Jacksonville, FL 32256-7504
904/443-1900

1320 S. Dixie Highway
Suite 501
Coral Gables, FL 33146
305/536-5521

Timberlake Federal Building
Suite 104
501 East Polk St.
Tampa, FL 33602-3945
813/228-2594

5601 Corporate Way
Suite 402
West Palm Beach, FL 33407
407/689-3922

Georgia
1720 Peachtree Road, NW
6th Floor
Atlanta, GA 30309
404/347-2441

Federal Building
52 North Main Street
Room 225
Statesboro, GA 30458
912/489-8719

Guam
Pacific Daily News Building
Room 508
238 O'Hara Street
Agana, Guam 96910
671/472-7277

Hawaii
300 Ala Moana Boulevard
Room 2213
Box 50207
Honolulu, HI 96850
808/541-2990

Idaho
1020 Main Street
Suite 290
Boise, ID 83702
208/334-1696

Illinois
500 W. Madison
Room 1250
Chicago, IL 60606
312/353-4528

511 W. Capitol Street
Suite 302
Springfield, IL 62704
217/492-4416

Indiana
429 N. Pennsylvania Street
Suite 100
Indianapolis, IN 46204-1873
317/226-7272

Iowa
210 Walnut Street
Room 749
Des Moines, IA 50309
515/284-4422

373 Collins Road, NE.
Room 100
Cedar Rapids, IA 52402-3167
319/393-8630

Kansas
110 E. Waterman Street
Wichita, KS 67202
316/269-6616

Kentucky
600 Dr. Martin Luther King, Jr. Place
Room 188
Louisville, KY 40202
502/582-5971

Louisiana
Ford-Fisk Building
1661 Canal Street
Suite 2000
New Orleans, LA 70112
504/589-2744

500 Fannin Street
Room 8A-08
Shreveport, LA 71101
318/226-5196

Maine
Federal Building
40 Western Avenue
Room 512
Augusta, ME 04330
207/622-8378

Maryland
Equitable Building
3rd Floor
10 N. Calvert Street
Baltimore, MD 21202
301/962-4392

Massachusetts
10 Causeway Street
Room 265
Boston, MA 02222-1093
617/565-5590

Federal Building & Courthouse
1550 Main Street
Room 212
Springfield, MA 01103
413/785-0268

Michigan
515 McNamara Building
477 Michigan Avenue
Detroit, MI 48226
313/226-6075

300 S. Front Street
Marquette, MI 49855
906/225-1108

Minnesota
610-C Butler Square
100 North 6th Street
Minneapolis, MN 55403-1563
612/370-2324

Mississippi
One Hancock Plaza
Suite 1001
Gulfport, MS 39501-7758
601/863-4449

First Jackson Centre
101 W. Capitol Street
Suite 400
Jackson, MS 39201
601/965-4378

Missouri
Lucas Place
323 West 8th St. S. 501
Kansas City, MO 64105
816/374-6708

815 Olive Street
Room 242
St. Louis, MO 63101
314/539-6600

620 S. Glenstone Street
Suite 110
Springfield, MO 65802-3200
417/864-7670

Montana
301 South Park
Drawer 10054
Room 528
Helena, MT 59626
406/449-5381

Nebraska
11145 Mill Valley Road
Omaha, NE 68154
402/221-4691

Nevada
301 East Stewart Street
Room 301
Box 7527 Downtown Station
Las Vegas, NV 89125
702/388-6611

50 S. Virginia Street
P.O. Box 3216
Room 238
Reno, NV 89505
702/784-5268

New Hampshire
55 Pleasant Street
Room 210, P.O. Box 1257
Concord, NH 03302-1257
603/225-1400

New Jersey
2600 Mt. Ephrain Avenue
Camden, NJ 08104
609/757-5183

Military Park Blvd.
60 Park Place
4th Floor
Newark, NJ 07102
201/645-2434

New Mexico
625 Silver Avenue, SW
Suite 320
Albuquerque, NM 87102
505/766-1870

New York
26 Federal Plaza
Room 3100
New York, NY 10278
212/264-4355

445 Broadway
Room 222
Albany, NY 12207
518/472-6300

111 W. Huron Street
Room 1311
Buffalo, NY 14202
716/846-4301

333 East Water Street
4th Floor
Elmira, NY 14901
607/734-8130

35 Pinelawn Road
Room 102E
Melville, NY 11747
516/454-0750

Federal Building
Room 410
100 State Street
Rochester, NY 14614
716/263-6700

Federal Building
P.O. Box 7317
Syracuse, NY 13261-7317
315/423-5383

North Carolina
222 S. Church Street
Suite 300
Charlotte, NC 28202
704/371-6563

North Dakota
Federal Building
Room 218
657 Second Avenue N.
Fargo, ND 58108-3086
701/239-5131

Ohio
AJC Federal Building
Room 317
1240 East 9th Street
Cleveland, OH 44199
216/522-4180

U.S. Courthouse
Federal Office Building
85 Marconi Boulevard
Room 512
Columbus, OH 43215-2887
614/469-6860

John Weld Peck Federal Building
550 Main Street
Room 5028
Cincinnati, OH 45202
513/684-2814

Oklahoma
200 NW 5th Street
Suite 670
Oklahoma City, OK 73102
405/231-4301

Oregon
222 SW Columbia Street
Suite 500
Portland, OR 97201-6605
503/326-2682

Pennsylvania
Allendale Square
Suite 201
475 Allendale Road
King of Prussia, PA 19406
215/962-3805

100 Chestnut Street
Suite 309
Harrisburg, PA 17101
717/782-3840

960 Penn Avenue
5th Floor
Pittsburgh, PA 15222
412/644-2780

Penn Place
20 N. Pennsylvania Avenue
Room 2327
Wilkes-Barre, PA 18703-3589
717/826-6497

Puerto Rico
Federico Degetau Federal Building
Room 691
Carlos Chardon Avenue
Hato Rey, PR 00918
809/766-5003

Rhode Island
380 Westminster Mall
5th Floor
Providence, RI 02903
401/528-4571

South Carolina
1835 Assembly Street
Room 358
P.O. Box 2786
Columbia, SC 29202-2786
803/765-5132

South Dakota
101 S. Main Avenue
Suite 101
Sioux Falls, SD 57102
605/336-4231

Tennessee
50 Vantage Way
Suite 201
Nashville, TN 37228-1550
615/736-5881

Texas
1100 Commerce Street
Room 3C-36
Dallas, TX 75242
214/767-0605

Federal Building
300 East 8th Street
Room 520
Austin, TX 78731
512/482-5288

819 Taylor Street
Room 10A27
Fort Worth, TX 76102
817/334-3777

Government Plaza Building
400 Mann Street
Suite 403
Corpus Christi, TX 78401
512/888-3331

10737 Gateway West
Suite 320
El Paso, TX 79902
915/540-5560

222 E. Van Buren Street
Suite 500
Harligen, TX 78550
512/427-8533

2525 Murworth
Suite 112
Houston, TX 77054
713/660-4401

1611 10th Street
Suite 200
Lubbock, TX 79401
806/743-7462

505 East Travis
Room 103
Marshall, TX 75670
214/935-5257

7400 Blanco Road
Suite 200
San Antonio, TX 78216
512/229-4535

Utah
125 South State Street
Room 2237
Salt Lake City, UT 84138-1195
801/524-5800

Vermont
87 State Street
Room 205
P.O. Box 605
Montpelier, VT 05601-0605
802/828-4422

Virginia
400 North 8th Street
Room 3015
P.O. Box 10126
Richmond, VA 23240
804/771-2617

Virgin Islands
Veterans Drive
Room 283
St. Thomas, VI 00801
809/774-8530

4C & 4D Estate Sion Farm
Room 7
St. Croix, VI 00820
809/778-5380

Washington
915 Second Avenue
Room 1792
Seattle, WA 98174-1088
206/442-5534

W. 601 First Avenue
10th Floor East
Spokane, WA 99204
509/353-2800

West Virginia
168 West Main Street
5th Floor
P.O. Box 1608
Clarksburg, WV 26301-1608
304/623-5631

550 Eagan Street
Room 309
Charleston, WV 25301
304/347-5220

Wisconsin
212 E. Washington Avenue
Room 213
Madison, WI 53703
608/264-5261

Henry S. Reuss Federal Plaza
310 W. Wisconsin Avenue
Suite 400
Milwaukee, WI 53203
414/297-3941

Wyoming
Federal Building
100 East B Street
Room 4001
P.O. Box 2839
Casper, WY 82602-2839
307/261-5761

SMALL BUSINESS DEVELOPMENT CENTERS (SBDCS)

Alabama
University of Alabama at
 Birmingham
1717 11th Avenue South, Suite 419
Birmingham, AL 35294
205/934-7260

Alaska
University of Alaska, Anchorage
430 W. 7th Avenue, Suite 110
Anchorage, AK 99501
907/274-7232

Arizona
Arizona SBDC Network
9215 N. Canyon Highway
Phoenix, AZ 85021
602/943-2311

Arkansas
University of Arkansas
100 South Main Street, Suite 401
Little Rock, AR 72201
501/324-9043

California
Department of Commerce
Small Business Development Center
801 K Street, Suite 1700
Sacramento, CA 95814
916/324-5068

Colorado
Small Business Development Center
Office of Business Development
1625 Broadway, Suite 1710
Denver, CO 80202
303/892-3809

Connecticut
University of Connecticut
368 Fairfield Road, SBA U-41,
Room 422
Storrs, CT 06269
203/486-4135

Delaware
University of Delaware
Purnell Hall, Suite 005
Newark, NJ 19716
302/831-2747

District of Columbia
Howard University
Small Business Development Center
2600 Sixth Street, Room 128
Washington, DC 20059
202/806-1550

Florida
University of West Florida
Florida SBDC Network
Building 76, Room 231
Pensacola, FL 32514
904/474-3016

Georgia
University of Georgia
1180 E. Broad Street
Athens, GA 30602
404/542-5760

Hawaii
Hawaii SBDC Network
University of Hawaii at Hilo
523 W. Lanikaula Street
Hilo, HI 96720
808/933-3515

Idaho
Boise State University
College of Business
1910 University Drive
Boise, ID 83725
208/835-1640

Illinois
Department of Commerce & Community Affairs
620 East Adams Street
Springfield, IL 62701
217/524-5856

Indiana
Indiana SBDC
One North Capital, Suite 420
Indianapolis, IN 46204
317/264-6871

Iowa
Iowa SBDC
Iowa State University
Chamberlain Building,
137 Lynn Avenue.
Ames, IA 50010
515/292-6351

Kansas
Wichita State University
1845 Fairmont, 21 Clinton Hall
Wichita, KS 67208
316/689-3193

Kentucky
University of Kentucky
225 Business and Economics
   Building
Lexington, KY 40506
606/257-7668

Louisiana
Northeast Louisiana University
College of Business
University Drive
Monroe, LA 71209
318/342-5506

Maine
University of Southern Maine
96 Falmouth Street
Portland, ME 04103
207/780-4420

Maryland
Maryland SBDC Network
State Administrative Office
Department of Economics &
Employment Development
217 East Redwood Street, 10th Floor
Baltimore, MD 21202
410/333-6996

Massachusetts
University of Massachusetts
205 School of Management
Amherst, MA 01003
413/545-6301

Michigan
Wayne State University
2727 Second Avenue
Detroit, MI 48201
313/577-4848

Minnesota
Dept. of Trade and Economic
Development
900 American Center Building
150 East Kellogg Blvd.
St. Paul, MN 55101
612/297-5770

Mississippi
Small Business Development Center
Old Chemistry Building,
Suite 216
University, MS 38677
601/232-5001

Missouri
MO SBDC
University of Missouri
300 University Place
Columbia, MO 65211
314/882-0344

Montana
Helena SBDC
Montana Department of Commerce
1424 Ninth Avenue
Helena, MT 59620
406/444-4780

Nebraska
University of Nebraska at Omaha
College of Business Administration
Building
60th and Dodge, Room 407
Omaha, NE 68182
402/554-2521

Nevada
University of Nevada, Reno
College of Business Administration,
Room 411
Reno, NV 89557
702/784-1717

New Hampshire
University of New Hampshire
108 McConnell Hall
Durham, NH 03824
603/862-2200

New Jersey
Small Business Development Center
Rutgers University
180 University Avenue
3rd Floor-Ackerson Hall
Newark, NJ 07102
201/648-5950

New Mexico
NMSBDC Lead Center
Santa Fe Community College
P.O. Box 4187
Santa Fe, NM 87502
505/438-1362

New York
State University of New York
SUNY Central Administration S-523
Albany, NY 12246
518/443-5398

North Carolina
University of North Carolina
4509 Creedmoor Road, Suite 201
Raleigh, NC 27612
919/733-4643

North Dakota
University of North Dakota
118 Gamble Hall, UND
Grand Forks, ND 58202
701/777-3700

Ohio
Small Business Development Center
77 South High Street
Columbus, OH 43226
614/466-2711

Oklahoma
Southeastern Oklahoma State
University
Station A Box 2584
Durant, OK 74701
405/924-0277

Oregon
Lane Community College
99 W. 10th Avenue, suite 216
Eugene, OR 97401
503/726-2250

Pennsylvania
University of Pennsylvania
The Wharton School
444 Vance Hall
Philadelphia, PA 19104
215/898-1219

Puerto Rico
University of Puerto Rico
Mayaguez Campus, Box 5253
Mayaguez, PR 00681
809/834-3590

Rhode Island
Bryant College SBDC
1150 Douglas Pike
Smithfield, RI 02917
401/232-6111

South Carolina
University of South Carolina
College of Business Administration
Columbia, SC 29208
803/777-4907

South Dakota
University of South Dakota
Business Research Bureau
414 E. Clark Street
Vermillion, SD 57069
605/677-5272

Tennessee
Memphis State University
Building 1, South Campus
Memphis, TN 38152
901/678-2500

Texas
Dallas SBDC
Bill J. Priest Institute for
 Economic Development
1402 Corinth Street
Dallas, TX 75215
214/565-5833

Utah
University of Utah
102 West 500 South, suite 315
Salt Lake City, UT 84101
801/581-7905

Vermont
Vermont SBDC
1 Blair Park, Suite 13
Williston, VT 05494
802/878-0181

Virginia
Virginia SBDC
Department of Economic
  Development
P.O. Box 798, 1021 East Cary Street
Richmond, VA 23219
804/371-8258

Virgin Islands
University of the Virgin Islands
P.O. Box 1087
St. Thomas, VI 00804
809/776-3206

Washington
Washington State University
245 Todd Hall
Pullman, WA 99164
509/335-1576

West Virginia
West Virginia SBDC
Governor's Office of Community
and Industrial Development
1115 Virginia Street
Charleston, WV 25301
304/348-2960

Wisconsin
University of Wisconsin
432 North Lake Street, Room 423
Madison, WI 53706
608/263-7794

Wyoming
WSBDC/State Network Office
111 W. 2nd Street, Suite 416
Casper, WY 82601
307/235-4825

Index